THE CHRISTIAN RESPONSE

THE CHRISTIAN RESPONSE

MICHEL QUOIST

GILL AND MACMILLAN

First published 1965
Gill and Macmillan Ltd
2 Belvedere Place
Dublin 1
and internationally through
association with the
Macmillan Publishers Group

7171 0027 8
Printing history
15 14 13

Printed and bound in Ireland at The Richview Press Ltd., Dublin

Contents

PART THREE MAN AND OTHERS

PART FOUR MAN AND HIS LIFE
IN CHRIST

Introduction

Mankind in Danger

The awesome problem of social injustice, particularly in what are termed the underdeveloped nations of the world, challenges the conscience of the human family today more so perhaps than at any other period. The untold suffering everywhere visible in the world is tangible evidence of the lamentable consequences of such a situation. But with the modern period another cancerous disease, more menacing still because it is even more devastating, made its appearance and, paradoxically enough, its first inroads have been made among those nations which are thought to be the most 'civilized.' The disease of which we speak involves the interior disintegration of man himself. The most outstanding thinkers of our day, those at any rate who still believe in the primacy of the spirit over matter, are united by their common concern, and even the human family itself is beginning to take cognizance of the danger.

Due to its incredible technological advances, the modern world now provides a radically altered setting for the human drama. Proud of his conquests and his newly won power over nature, modern man seems each day to make further advances in his subjugation of the forces of nature. However, as man's mastery over nature accelerates by virtue of his expanding scientific and technological knowledge, his mastery over the interior universe of his own personality diminishes. As he penetrates deeper into the worlds revealed by his microscopes and his telescopes, he becomes increasingly unintelligible to himself. In his determination to subject the whole cosmos to his own will man has rendered himself incapable of directing his own life. Because modern man has been set free from the tyranny of nature by his power to control its forces, we would expect him to have consecrated himself more unreservedly to the things of the spirit; however, like a caged animal, nature has turned on its supposed master, making him its slave and at the same time subjecting the spirit to its own whims.

When man forsakes the spirit, he loses all else in its wake. Man is no longer deserving of the name, for a truly human life always implies the primacy of spirit over the world of matter. It is the spirit which enables man to plan and accomplish the subjection of nature, and the cities arising majestically from our hills and plains, together with the machinery pouring out of our factories, bear eloquent witness to man's spiritual prowess. Sculpture, music, art, and literature are all monuments to the human spirit's capacity to engender the beautiful. Love is possible only where spirit is to be found, whether this love embraces but two persons, a whole community, or even the whole of the human family. But when the values of the spirit are menaced, the whole human personality is endangered, for man's desires, machines, cities, and world, turn against him with a vengeance, determined to crush him beneath their accumulated weight. Thus man sees his vaunted power over nature slip from his hands once again, for he has ceased to be a human person. Today we find ourselves confronted with the gigantic task of undoing or rather of re-doing what has already been done.

Even a mere nodding acquaintance with history shows us that one proud civilization after another has seen its star of fortune wane and finally disappear. If we look back down the long and tortuous road of human history we will find that very few of these civilizations fell beneath the blows of an invading conqueror; by far the majority acted as their own executioners, gradually rotting from inside and finally collapsing. We take great pride in the Western tradition and in Western civilization, and in order to preserve our Western heritage we were willing to take part in the wholesale slaughter of millions, and in the infliction of untold suffering upon many millions more. In order to preserve this heritage the great nations of the world have armed themselves, stockpiling weapons capable of annihilating whole continents.

Unquestionably our civilization stands at a critical juncture in human history, but the enemy is threatening to erupt from within the human heart rather than from outside our national boundaries. The disease is already at work within, inexorably accomplishing its work of destruction. And the modern world becomes its enthusiastic accomplice when it holds out to human weakness the lure of easy pleasure, and to the human spirit the lure of a self-sufficient autonomy.

Having sown the wind we are now reaping the whirlwind. If we would gauge the extent of our own moral failure we need only look to the increase in juvenile delinquency, which is reaching such proportions in some 'developed' countries that it is becoming a veritable scourge. The increased incidence of mental illness and emotional disorders offers us a further indication of the tragic situation in which modern man finds himself; primitives in many areas have need of doctors for their bodies, but the *civilized* have need of an ever larger army of psychoanalysts, psychotherapists, and psychiatrists in order to safeguard their mental balance. Perhaps in the not-too-distant future man will set foot on neighbouring planets.

But what will be the interior state of this man? The whole of the human family must give ear to the solemn and still contemporaneous warning of Jesus Christ: 'What does it profit a man to gain the whole world and suffer the loss of his immortal soul?'

Let me hasten to add, however, that we not only do not have the right to bridle the staggering progress made in modern times, but we have an urgent obligation to work at this task rather than run from it. Let us not forget, however, that we will have laboured in vain if we do not at the same time strive to make man aware that he possesses an immortal spirit. We have to remake man so that the universe may be remade through him, in conformity with a pattern of order and love.

As our opportunities for a fuller life and greater enjoyment multiply, it becomes all the more imperative that we understand that these are only means to a higher end. We stand in need of a new spiritual strength if we are not to become their slaves. We have need of a more profound love if we are to avoid monopolizing these things for ourselves to the exclusion of our brothers. It is a simple fact of experience in the modern world that the greater the complexity the more urgent the need for technical know-how, and hence as the world grows in complexity we stand in need of a profounder life of the spirit if we are to build a stable world. If man and the universe in which he lives are to attain their fulfilment, it will not be sufficient any longer simply to help man rediscover his soul, it is essential that he be offered that 'soul-supplement' for which Bergson was already calling at the turn of the century.

But let us go still further. If the human spirit is today reeling under the blow dealt it by the world of technology, it is precisely because man has forgotten, ignored, or denied his God. Man's freedom can choose one or two poles: either he can attach himself to God by detaching himself from the material, or else he can attach himself to the material by detaching himself from God. No man can serve two masters. In short, if man is presently in critical condition, it is because he has opted for self and the material over and against God and the spiritual.

The world holds a fatal fascination for modern man. Man's productivity is constantly on the increase, and yet in his continual dissatisfaction he devours what he has made without ever attaining fulfilment. He is trapped in a vicious circle in which his needs increase more rapidly than his power to produce novelties to satisfy them. Attempting to reap the fruits of his material progress, he finds himself kneeling before these idols which he has created and which are the new gods of the modern world. Divided at the deepest level of his personality, condemned to continual struggle against his brothers, modern man grasps at every straw promising material well-being and tries to cling to it for his own personal enjoyment.

In spite of his failure, modern man stands admiringly before the world in which he sees himself and his genius mirrored. Bedazzled by his technological accomplishments, he forgets to look to the God to whom all glory belongs. As his power over the forces of nature widens, modern man loses sight of the omnipotence of God, making idols of the good things of this world or seeing himself as the god of creation. In this way *civilized* man abandons the one, true God, and in spite of his declarations to the contrary, builds a world from which God is excluded. A subtle form of atheism perhaps, but quite as effective as its more blatant manifestations.

The words of Jesus Christ, who entered human history as the Father's ambassador that he might bring salvation to man and to his world, are still relevant in the modern period:

'I am the Way, the Truth, and the Life . . .

Without me you can do nothing . . .

I am come that you may have life and have it more abundantly . . .

I am the resurrection and the life, every man who lives and believes in me will never taste death . . .

My peace I leave with you, my peace I give unto you, not as the world gives do I give unto you. . . .'

If man and the world in which he lives are to find fulfilment, it will be necessary not only to help modern man rediscover his soul, not only to help him to find a 'soul-supplement,' but it is imperative that he be led back to Jesus Christ. Otherwise tomorrow man will have ceased to be himself, for today man finds himself in critical condition.

It is because we are convinced of the reality of this crisis, this danger which threatens to destroy man and which has already begun its work, that we have written these pages. It is hoped that they may cause some to stop for a few moments to re-evaluate their present values and to renew their commitment to the primacy of the spirit in human life. Ours is a small enough undertaking in comparison with the magnitude of the task which challenges us. Better, nonetheless, to light one candle than to curse the darkness. God, to whom this work is humbly entrusted, will know how to make the best use of it if he wills to and if we place ourselves completely at his service.

The Meaning of Success

In reply to a questionnaire on the attitudes of the present generation circulated by the French Institute of Public Opinion for the newspaper *Vie catholique illustrée*, 90% of the young people interviewed said that it was important to them to be 'successful in life,' 88% that it was important to them to get a good job, and 59% that it was important to them to get married and to be able to provide security for their families. It goes without saying that all of us want to make a success of our lives. But for what sort of success are we aiming? All too often it is merely material success. It will be our task in this book to offer some reflections on what is real success, and what it means to succeed in living the Christian life.

From the point of view of the unbeliever, this kind of success may at times appear to be outright failure. We use *at times* advisedly, for we should keep in mind the words of our Lord promising a hundredfold return to those who follow him, a hundredfold return not only hereafter, but here as well. We should never forget that we are actually obliged to do all in our power to make a success of our lives and the world in which we live. Otherwise, we can not expect the Lord to bless us with the graces we need to succeed supernaturally—our ultimate fulfilment.

Our discussion in these pages will centre on man, for in the last analysis the transformation of the whole cosmos hinges upon the transformation of man. And even though we believe it foolish to think that a change in the social **structure** will suffice of itself to transform man, nonetheless we do believe that it is equally foolish to change man without at the same time attempting to change the social institutions in the context of which his life is lived. Both these tasks have to be undertaken at one and the same time with equal earnestness and commitment. It is a serious but common error today to think that those interested in the apostolate should stand in the wings until their *formation* is complete before seeking to exert any influence on their world. We have lost sight of the fact that it is only through acting in and on our world that we can be properly and fully formed, and it is only through genuine love of our brothers that we give tangible evidence of our love for Christ. From both a natural and supernatural perspective man can not make a success of his life unless he is working to make a success of his world.

The present work makes no claim to be an authoritative rule book for the proper conduct of human life or for that matter the Christian life either. Rather, as we have already mentioned, we wish only to offer some reflections on the role the Christian must play in perfecting his own personality and the world in which he lives. These reflections are grouped into chapters, some of which are related to one another, some of which are not. Since we had no intention of presenting a complete system of thought, we hope that we shall not be accused of having failed to deal with some important questions. The same holds true for the individual 'chapters,' for in them only certain aspects of a topic are developed, whereas others are intentionally left in the background.

For the sake of clarity, however, we have brought these reflections together under four general headings: Man, Man and His Life, Man and Others, Man and His Life in Christ. These divisions are not to be considered as airtight compartments; in fact, each chapter should be seen in the light of all the others, and to keep this point in mind we have often had recourse to cross references. We also wish to underline the fact that we have no intention of relegating the relationship between ourselves and Christ to a particular aspect of human life. On the contrary, we hope to have succeeded in showing that all our efforts to complete ourselves, our lives, and our world, should be considered inseparably linked with our efforts in Christ to construct the Kingdom of the Father.

We have chosen certain themes to the exclusion of others and certain aspects of these themes to the exclusion of others in order to meet the pressing needs of the contemporary world in which we are placed. It should be made quite clear that this book was not written from the window of an ivory tower, but rather we have tried throughout to keep vitally in touch with the real world, in the belief that it is God himself who speaks to us in the need we see about us. Perhaps you are seeking light on a particular problem, perhaps you are seeking advice on a particular aspect of your life. Each of you is demanding a reply to his own particular questions. Today it was found necessary to reply in this way, tomorrow it will be necessary to reply in a different way in response to different questions posed by different questioners. We have tried to be succinct, direct, and intelligible to modern readers. Hence we have used the ordinary language of everyday life to express truths which are themselves eternal and unchangeable. We have frequently employed the second person in the hope that the reader will thus be led to apply to himself personally these reflections which we have first addressed to ourselves. Modern men unfortunately do not have the time to read extended treatises, but who is so busy that he can not find a few spare moments in the day to reflect on a few lines? We earnestly hope that the reader will be led to reflect on the questions discussed here in such a way that he will be forced to look into his own life and reconsider his stance towards himself, his world and his God.

Anyone who takes the time to reflect briefly on a particular text (using it simply as a point of departure), and tries to determine its applicability to his own personal life, and tries as well to be attentive to the voice of God in his heart, can not help but come to a deeper appreciation of the spiritual dimension of his life and the place of Christ, his Saviour, in that life. May some of you at least find these few moments of reflection a source of help. May we in our own small way help you to make a success of your lives and the world in which you live.

PART ONE

Man

A Man has to Stand on his Feet

Man dreams of becoming the master of his destiny and he is right in so doing, for he transcends the merely natural order through his ability to know both himself and the world in which he lives. He is capable of making value-judgments and of directing his life in conformity with self-created ideals. However, many men who think that they are the sole masters of their activity are in fact slaves to their own bodies and to their emotions. They have not yet succeeded in harnessing their instinctual drives. Either they do not clearly perceive their true situation or else they assume that their own strength is sufficient for a successful life.

Few men have what could be termed a well-integrated psychological life. Few have achieved a harmonious ordering of the diverse elements of their human make-up. If very few have attained a perfect balance, it is either because they have not been encouraged to strive for self-integration (this should be the aim of education) or because they have never really worked at the task themselves (either as adolescents or as adults). In some instances a complex of influences have converged in bringing about the individual's downfall: personal inadequacies, the corrupting example of others, environmental circumstances . . . Few men are in fact worthy of the name.

The well-integrated man might be defined as the man who has brought the spiritual, the emotional and the physical into harmony. These three levels [1] are bound up in and influence one another but we have to respect their hierarchical structure; the physical is the least noble of the three, the spiritual the most exalted. Unless a value-order is preserved, man is perverted.

Some men try to live standing on their heads. This ultimately proves to be an impossible stance for any man worthy of the name. You try to live standing on your head when the physical—your body—gets the upper hand and is allowed to assume command. Such a topsy-turvy situation can result from sensuality in all its various forms, or from illness when it is permitted to cripple the spirit instead of being used for personal growth and offered to God. If your body makes all the decisions and gives all the orders, and if you obey, the physical can effectively destroy every other dimension of your personality. Your emotional life will be blunted and your spiritual life will be stifled and ultimately will become anaemic.

Perhaps your body has not yet taken complete and definitive control of your life. Perhaps; but if you watch yourself attentively you will be surprised to find yourself standing on your head all too often: that irresistible urge to eat and drink just to gratify your desire; that inertia which refuses to let you get up in the morning or to let you do anything once you are up; that physical excitement which is sought with no other end in view than self-satisfaction; that sexual pleasure which you desire simply for its own sake. Up on your feet—be a man!

Some people just barely crawl along, for emotion has taken the upper hand in their lives. Emotion has assumed control of your life when affection turns to passion and makes you 'lose your head' because reason has been submerged beneath the waves of passion. When emotion rules, it paralyzes the spirit and having banished freedom it holds the personality captive to its whims. Perhaps you have not yet become the hopeless slave of your emotional whims. Perhaps; but do they not have the last say all too frequently? They do if the truth of an opinion depends upon your feelings towards the person who holds it, or if your ability to work under one teacher rather than another depends on his attitude towards you, or if you're ready to give up because nobody appreciates you, or if you pray only when you're 'in form,' and when you're not, you simply don't bother. You're not standing on your feet, you're crawling, you're a slave.

The man who stands on his feet is the man in whom the spiritual holds the reins over the emotional and physical levels with complete freedom to direct them for the total good of the personality. Neither the physical nor the emotional is to be treated with contempt for they are both good and both have their place because they are the work of God, but the spirit is their master and must give direction to them both. The spirit is lord, they are servants. It is right that you should give expression to your emotions and to your physical desires; [2] they have a part to play in your life, if they are given proper direction. They are headstrong steeds and you have to keep the reins firmly in hand; they are like a car—you have to keep your hands on the wheel. If your mount bolts, or if you lose control of your car, you're in for trouble.

Some people are 'floaters'—they don't have their feet on the ground. You float: when you take your dreams for the real thing, when you spend your time thinking up all sorts of plans which you never do anything about, when you stubbornly refuse to give in to others, when you won't accept yourself as you are, nor others as they are, nor your circumstances. . . . You float when, because of your fear of life as it really is, you fail to be generous or when, to flatter your vanity, you let yourself be carried away by day-dreams. To dream your life away is not the same thing as to live it. You are right in hitching your wagon to a star to spur yourself on, but never to escape from reality.

If you want to have an integrated personality and to stand on your feet, you have to keep reminding yourself of the different levels of your make-up and their proper order, then keep a close watch over yourself in your relations with others, in your various activities, and in your attitudes. . . . What made you decide to do that, to act in this way or react in that? To realize that it wasn't really you who issued the order is already a victory for the spirit. The spirit is then no longer a blind victim, but is set free and assumes once again its directive role in your life.

You can't stand on your feet through your efforts alone; your body weighs you down too much, your emotions are much too sensitive. You stand in need of a Force which will draw you toward the heights and sustain your flight. This Force has to transform your inner life. If you open your soul to God you will be strong with his strength, and you will hold both your emotional and physical life in your own hands because he is holding you in his. If you reject God you will find that you are only half a man because the whole man in the eternal design of God is a man standing on his feet and made divine.

The two Dimensions of Man

*The absolutely self-sufficient man needing no one outside
himself is, in reality, inconceivable. If you want to
make a success of your life you have to open the doors of
your personality freely and unreservedly to the God who in
his great love is not content simply to create you but
desires as well to become one with you in your life,
transforming that life through the gift of his own life.
You should never think of yourself as an island cut off from
the mainland, for you are inevitably related to all men
and you must become one with them through the free gift
of your love if you would achieve fulfilment.
Only the saint is the totally fulfilled man for, set free
from the bondage of self, he is able to welcome into his
life both his God and his brothers.*

A man worthy of the name is a man who can stand on his
feet and face reality. He's the man who has allowed the
Lord to transform his life at the deepest levels of his
personality. 'It is no longer I who live but Christ who lives
in me.' [1] This is what we may term man's vertical dimension, his relationship to God. A man worthy of the name is
the man who has opened his heart to all his brothers, no
matter where or when they played their part in the drama
of human existence, so that he might be one with them in
their problems and concerns, their hopes and aspirations.
This is man's horizontal dimension, his relationship to
others. If you're not functioning two-dimensionally you're

not a man worthy of the name, you're hardly half a man.

Men aren't merely thrown together like potatoes in a sack; they are persons and hence they are related one to another. You are a member of the human family, and so every man is related to you in some way precisely because he too belongs to this same human family. You will never know yourself completely until you know all other men. You will reach maturity only when you become one with all of them, for all are members of the body of the human family just as you are.

The child becomes an adolescent when he achieves self-consciousness; the adolescent attains adulthood when he becomes other-conscious. Don't be afraid of being self-conscious, for if you are then you'll recognize your own limitations, and once you recognize your own limitations, you are ready to welcome others into your life so that they can enrich your personality and make your life fully human. It's difficult to see how any man can live in isolation without being the worse for it.

Modern psychology only reinforces the clear teaching of the gospels when it tells us that man is torn between two opposing attitudes which he can adopt in regard to his life in the world. The one is basically expansive and relational and is called love; it is love which draws us out of ourselves and makes us community builders, all the way from the community of the family to the community of mankind. The other is regressive and isolating and is called egoism; it is egoism which leads us to retreat from life into ourselves and tries to convince us that we can go it alone. There is no more deceptive illusion. No matter how talented you may be, if you try to go it alone, you will never attain full maturity. And if you wish to be enriched by others you have to become one with them, which is just another way of saying that you have to love them. The more you love others, the more adult you will become.

If this is your attitude: every man for himself, *my* interests come first (*my* studies, *my* family, *my* future, *my* well-being . . .), I haven't time for anyone else, I'm not going to get involved in other people's business (that is, I'll have nothing to do with those with whom I go to school, or with whom I work, or who live in my neighbourhood . . .), then do something about it, because if you don't you will never grow up, you'll be a spiritual dwarf all your life. You have to become a link in a chain of relationships. First of all you have to link yourself with those who form your daily contacts: your family, your neighbours, your school acquaintances, your fellow workers, your sporting companions. If no spirit of community exists between you and them, if you want to remain an outsider, how is the whole human race to be joined in community? To go it alone is to fail as a human person; to go it alone is, in the plan of the Father, to renounce salvation.

To encounter others you first have to see them: that means you have to open your eyes! To be able to welcome others into your life, you first must have room in your life for them: that means you have to empty yourself! To be able to become one with others you have to get out of yourself: that means you have to learn self-forgetfulness and generosity. You have to become one with those who do not form your circle of acquaintances in a spiritual way: you have to meet them by learning about their lives and problems, you have to carry them in your heart through love. Learn about their problems, their sufferings, their joys . . . through the newspaper, the radio, the cinema, television, reading, lectures and travel. Gradually enlarge your field of vision, your awareness of the lives of your brothers, until it extends to every corner of the world.

A man's greatness is to be measured by his capacity for communion with others. God is a community of persons and he has created you in his image, not as an isolated individual, but as a person whom he invited to a communal life with himself and with the whole human family. Salvation history bears witness to God's loving concern for the whole community of men, for he first made a covenant with a *people*, and then established a *church*. In the mind of God the human family is a unity, a family of sons with but one Father. It is sin which 'has scattered the sons of men over the face of the earth.'[2] Each of us must help to re-create the original unity of the human family. We are simply incomplete as long as a single one of our brothers remains an outsider and as long as we are unable to call ourselves, with perfect sincerity, a brother to all.

There are some who think that God can be eliminated from the picture, that it is sufficient for a man to strive for an all-embracing brotherhood of man without God. Is it really possible to speak of brothers where there is no father, and who can assume the role of Father of all men save the Creator of all? If you truly want to be the brother of all men you have to accept your role as son, you have to receive and live the life of God—and the more fully you are a son, the more fully you will be a brother.

There are some who think it suffices to become one with God without bothering about their brothers. If you really want to be a son of the Father, you have to accept your role as a brother of all his other sons. When you reject a brother, you reject the Father as well, you are in fact denying the Father. As a result, you are blighting any possibility for spiritual growth. If you want to achieve fulfilment, you have to love your brothers: 'We know that we have passed from death to life, because we love the brethren. He who does not love abides in death.' [3] The more completely and profoundly you love other men, to that degree will you 'pass from death to life'; the further you withdraw from them, to that degree will you destroy your personality in passing 'from life to death.'

Open yourself to God and to your brothers. Seek out your God and your brothers, become one with them both. These two movements are not mutually exclusive; on the contrary, they complement one another and guarantee each other's authenticity. Through the Incarnation and the Redemption Christ has made the human family his Mystical Body: in becoming one with the Lord you become one with the whole human family for you can not receive the Head without at the same time receiving the members; in uniting yourself to your fellow men you encounter the Lord, for you can not welcome the members into your life without at the same time welcoming the Head. The sacrifice of self-love is the only means to growth in the love of God and your fellow man. If you are willing to make the sacrifice, then and only then will you become a man.

The Divided Man

The modern world in which we live is faced with a threat far more serious than that of a nuclear holocaust: the total devastation of man's interior life through a process

*of psychological and spiritual fragmentation. It may be
true that modern man holds a tighter rein over the forces
of nature but at the same time he has lost possession of his
own personality in his extreme extroversion.
Man must once again become a unified whole if he truly
wishes to live and act as a human person.*

A tree nourishes its life by drawing into itself various minerals from outside itself. It then makes these lifeless elements partakers of its own life, thus elevating them to a new higher level of existence: that of plant life. In the animal we find both the mineral and the vegetative present as constitutive elements, but again these are elevated to a new level of existence: that of animal life. The life of man is both vegetative and animal but these levels are subordinated and transformed by reason and freedom and put at the service of human life. If you would live a truly human life the spirit must dominate and order the instinctual and sentient levels of your existence. Where the spirit holds the primacy, there a truly human life is lived; where instinct holds the primacy, there human life is reduced to mere animal existence. The choice rests ultimately with you. Every sin bears witness to the triumph of man's lower nature over his higher; in the process man is made less human because the hierarchical order of reality has been turned upside down.

Your geranium and your dog have attained their proper perfection, limited as it may be, without making any personal contribution. But your dignity consists precisely in the role you must play in the attainment of your own perfection. You are incomplete, you have to take a hand in your own self-completion. This is the highest expression of your creativity.

A wheel whose spokes have come loose from the hub is hardly worthy of the name. The same holds true for an atom if the electrons 'get free' of the nucleus. Unless the spirit draws together into harmony all of man's physical and spiritual energies, a man is rendered unworthy of the name. Man is divided against himself when his sense life gets out of hand, when emotions, feelings, and imagination are in open revolt, when the unbridled instincts thunder out of control, when the spirit is no longer able to impose its rule, when the ideal is compromised for the sake of a momentary desire. In these circumstances it is no longer possible to speak of man, for that which makes life truly human has been effectively crushed in the revolution. To become a man it is necessary to draw together again all your energies, it is necessary to re-order them in the light of their authentic place in human life, it is necessary to place them at the service of the spirit.

If you want to attain self-completion, it is not sufficient simply to establish a hierarchical order among the diverse elements of your make-up.[1] For they must also be unified by the spirit into a coherent and purposive personal life. It is relatively easy to keep rein on a tired old nag, but it is difficult to do so when your steed is young and high-spirited. It is far more difficult however to do so when you're driving a team of six thoroughbreds. But, if you can do it, a team of horses will take you farther faster. It's not an easy task to bring harmony and unity into the life of modern man. The lower instincts, which are very often overdeveloped and frequently the hapless victims of external stimuli, are very hard for the spirit to control directly. Today, however, more so than ever before, the man who can accomplish the task will find the sphere of his influence immeasurably broadened.

If you want to put your *entire* self into what you do, if you want to give yourself *completely*, if you want to be *fully* at the service of others, if you want to love with *all* your heart, if you want to pray with *total* attention, then strive to take perfect possession of your body, your heart, your spirit, and all their robust vitality, strive to take possession of yourself and then you will be able to say: *I* am acting, *I* am giving myself, *I* am at the service of others, *I* am loving, *I* am praying. To live life at its fullest means to draw together all your energies, to unify them, to personalize them, and to concentrate them on the present moment just as a magnifying glass concentrates the rays of the sun on a particular spot.[2] The man who has unified his own personal life is able to bring tranquillity and peace into the lives of others. If you want to be a bearer of peace to others you first have to establish peace in your own interior household.

Would a cyclist show much enthusiasm if he didn't know where he was going? If the builders didn't have a plan how could the house ever reach completion? How can you hope to bring harmony and unity into your life if you don't know why or how? You have to have a master plan in your head and in your heart, a plan which will draw your life into a unified pattern. Your goal and your plan are a living person: Jesus Christ. It is only in him and through him that you will be able to build a unified personal life for he has come to re-establish the harmony of both man and his world. It is because of sin that man and his times are out of joint. Only the Redemption alive in man's heart can balance his life properly and save him. Welcome the Saviour into the inner depths of your personality. Working from this centre the divine visitor in his love will begin to bring together into unity all of your energies, you will begin to take shape as an authentic human person. In him, you will become not only a man standing on his feet, not only a man whose activity radiates from a unified personality, but a man made divine.

The Well-Ordered Man

We have to love "with our whole heart" and "with our whole strength." Such is the Lord's commandment. Consequently no aspect of our human make-up is to be treated with contempt, let alone stifled. Each element must then be seen in its proper place, welcomed into our lives and given direction. The contemporary world seems to be at a loss as to how it is to deal with its emotional life. In some cases, when the emotions have been denied an outlet, they take their revenge in the form of mental disorders. In other cases, when allowed to run riot, they distort the individual's sense of values and cripple his ability to act effectively.
It would also seem that today altogether too large an area of man's moral life has become the province of naked will power, for the will must function in union with the intelligence and with the co-operation of the emotions. It is only by harmonizing in Christ all the levels of our human make-up that we can build a balanced personality and develop a sound and stable spiritual life.

Each level of our human make-up[1] gives evidence of possessing its own peculiar needs and drives. All of these are essentially good in themselves, and so they can not simply be stifled. However, all of them have also been affected by the ravages of man's sin and so they can not simply be allowed to run loose. Just as a tame animal can revert to a state of savagery if it is left to run wild, so too you will be reduced to mere animal existence if your instinctual and emotional drives are left unchecked. When water is held back by a dam its potential power is thereby considerably increased. It can then serve as a bearer of life when it is properly channelled, for purposes of irrigation for example. When the spirit holds your instinctual drives in check and gives them proper direction these can then be put at the service of your faith-ideals. If you hold back the guiding hand of the spirit, your instinctual drives will soon be out of control. You have to decide whether spirit or instinct will hold the reins over your life.

If you reject the one, true God, you will inevitably become the worshipper of idols, for man can not live without a god to worship. Unless you cultivate the life of the spirit, you will become the plaything of your instinctual drives. If you close the door to every noble aspiration, you will ultimately become the slave of instinct.

Don't make sacrifices simply to keep yourself in shape, or to strengthen your will power, or to get to the top, because pride will vitiate your good intentions and your frustrated emotions will try to satisfy the cravings of instinct. Some supposedly virtuous acts are actually repressive in character, and so it is very often better to aim at greater purity of heart with less external asceticism. Don't just trim the tree which has begun to grow wild but graft new shoots onto it so that it can become fruitful again. Don't just make sacrifices, but "sublimate" your instinctual drives so that your life as a human person and as a Christian may develop to maturity. When you do make sacrifices let them be sacrifices inspired by love; when you do deny yourself let it be for the purpose of welcoming your brothers and your God into your life. Death to self should aim solely at a richer, fuller life in Christ. The goal of human life is not death but resurrection.

Perhaps you find your emotions particularly difficult to control.[2] Nonetheless don't try to repress them, they can provide the basis for an extraordinarily rich life; they offer you the privilege of being deeply moved at the sight of beauty or by the suffering of another, of knowing the keen pleasure afforded by a work of art or by the joy of a close friend, of entering with facility into companionship with others and of profoundly appreciating the situations in which life places you and the persons with whom you come in contact, of personally experiencing the powerful invitation of generosity prompted by affection.

Emotion and intelligence should make life's journey as friends; working in isolation from one another, both will tend to be shallow and superficial. If you give your dog a savage beating every time he barks, he will soon keep himself hidden in his kennel. If you keep your emotions continually pent up within yourself, they may eventually find it difficult to function normally. A child who is treated with cruelty and injustice gradually becomes a sneak and a liar, and eventually a thief; he takes his revenge by being underhanded. Beware of your emotions; if you are brutal with them, they may go underground but they will keep up their resistance. Thus reduced to guerrilla warfare, your emotions will stifle the life of intelligence and weaken its capacity to make valid value judgments.[3] They will also tend to join forces with the weak spot in your character (a tendency to authoritarianism or self-will or violence or impurity, etc.) so as to give it added strength. One day, unexpectedly, the volcano will erupt.

A child will close his eyes when he sees something which frightens him. For a few moments he feels reassured, but unfortunately the difficulty remains. If, because of your fears, you refuse to recognize your emotional reactions for what they are, you are not merely suppressing them but your are 'repressing' them. When you cover over a wound without taking care of it, it quickly infects and spreads. You have to see what's wrong and take care of it. If you are hurt emotionally by a sharp rebuff, or someone's coarseness, or a false friend, or a failure of some kind, don't be embarrassed by the spontaneous emotional reaction which you experience, it's nothing to be ashamed of; don't play the 'tough guy' by pretending that nothing has happened; it's not a weakness; don't just put it aside contemptuously; it's not without significance.

Be honest with yourself and try to discover why you reacted the way you did: then, and only then, will you be able to do something about it. In this way every upsurge of emotion can lead to a deeper self-knowledge and self-possession, provided that you recognize it for what it is and accept it for what it is and then try to deal with it. Anyone knows that it is impossible to work the land while it's covered by water. Likewise, if you're submerged beneath a flood of emotion, your thinking, your sense of values, and your activity will be confused until your emotions have subsided and things are back to normal.

During the week following a football match the players talk over the various moves and then criticize them. It is a common practice for the wise teacher to take aside a troublesome student in order to discuss any problems he may be having and to offer his advice. If you want to educate your emotions, you have to take a long, hard look at the place they occupy in your life at present and you have to make every effort to set things in order. When you are upset by something that has happened or by someone whom you know, stop for a moment: look at the situation *objectively* and try to see what role intelligence has played in your reaction and also what role emotion has played. Accept both the situation and your reaction to it, then evaluate it calmly and decide what attitude you should take in the light of your faith-ideals.[4]

Don't just try to learn to recognize and accept your emotions for what they are, but learn also to offer all to God, whether it be joy or sorrow, or even sin. It is in this way that you will grow to maturity and gradually you will have put the whole of your life in God's keeping.[5]

The authentic spiritual life is not one devoid of all emotion, but rather one in which emotion is given its proper orientation by the spirit and which is purified by grace so that it no longer opposes itself to the divine life within man. Christ has not come to stifle all your emotional drives and needs; rather he has come to put them in their proper place in your life and even to divinize them. You must love your God and your brothers 'with your whole heart and your whole strength, and your whole self.' But this self must first be made divine. 'Delight in the Lord and he will give thee what thy heart desires.'[6]

The Vocation of Woman

Some men still hold women in contempt. Some women
regret the fact that they are women and demand a
'promotion,' which in point of fact is nothing more than
an artificial equality, the attainment of what are considered
to be masculine privileges. In reality, men and women
are fully equal in dignity, but they do nonetheless differ
and so complement one another.
The modern world is plainly a man's world.
Woman does not play in that world the role she should.
On the one hand, she must rediscover her uniqueness
through the cultivation of her peculiarly feminine
characteristics, otherwise she can not hope to fulfil her
mission in a man's life; on the other hand, she must take an
active part in forming the world in which she lives.
Confronted as we are by the overwhelming onrush of
materialism, it is woman's task and responsibility to bear
witness to and be the mother of the human element
in civilization.

From a Christian point of view, there exists an absolute
equality between man and woman: they are both creatures
of God, both have been redeemed by Christ, both are
children of God, both are called to the same supernatural
destiny. St Paul says: 'There is neither Jew nor Greek;
there is neither slave nor freeman; there is neither male nor
female. For you are all one in Christ Jesus.'[1]

It is incorrect to say, at least without qualification, that a
woman's place is in the home, and a man's is in the world,

for the command to 'fill the earth and subdue it'[2] was addressed to both man and woman alike. It was to both that the Creator gave the responsibility for future generations and for the completion of his work of creation. Consequently, woman can not be denied her rightful place in any area of human activity.

It is also, however, incorrect to say, at least without qualification, that men and woman are equal and so they should work at the very same tasks indiscriminately; for God said to woman: 'In sorrow shalt thou bring forth children,' and to man he said: 'In the sweat of thy face shalt thou eat bread.' Man and woman have the same essential dignity, the same work to bring to completion, the same supernatural destiny, but their functions differ and complement one another. Woman's vocation lies with the increase of the human family, man's with the building of the universe. Woman's life is centred on the community, whereas man's is centred on the life of the city, and their differing physical and psychological make-ups reveal the basic orientation of their vocations. These constitute a sign of God's will in their regard.

The seed remains incomplete if there is no soil to receive it. Man is incomplete if he finds no woman to receive him and woman is equally incomplete if she finds no man to make her fruitful. Man has need of woman for his self-completion, and so let her remain and become still more a woman. Woman has need of man for her self-completion, and so let him be and become still more a man. When a girl becomes a tomboy and a boy becomes effeminate, the relationship which should exist between young people is perverted. This situation can ultimately lead to unstable homes and sometimes even to failure of marriage. A sound society can not be built on an uncertain foundation.

If woman would fulfil her mission she must always be in some sense a *mystery* to man. This she has not succeeded in doing in the modern world, thus bearing witness to her failure to remain a woman. Today many women are shallow, superficial caricatures of true womanhood. If a woman gives only her body to a man, she can not fully satisfy his craving, she can not be fully loved by him. For the need a man has for a woman's body is only the external sign of the need he experiences for spiritual union with her. If a woman gives herself body and soul to a man, then she truly fulfils him and experiences authentic love herself. But man needs still more, for he needs to become aware through her of human inadequacy: 'I am incapable of giving you all that you crave'; for besides the body and soul of a woman, man has need of the infinity of God. It is only in and through Christ that woman can accomplish in its entirety her vocation to give ALL to man and to the world.

In one form or other woman must always give herself in marriage to man; neither can attain self-fulfilment nor can life be brought into the world without their mutual union and co-operation in the home, in society, and in the Church. Physically or spiritually, woman must make a gift of her life; in the profoundest sense her vocation in the world is to be a mother. Virginity does not limit the possibilities of this vocation, for the fruitfulness of the spirit is greater than that of the flesh. Spiritually woman must ever remain a virgin, keeping nothing for herself, possessing nothing of her own, unreservedly generous in the total gift of her life. A child brought up without one of his parents is irremediably marked by the experience, but it is better that he be without a father than a mother. The modern world was built without woman. It suffers from the lack of a mother. It is inhuman as a result.

In adolescence a man discovers that he is unique and irreplaceable. Upon attaining maturity a man discovers that he is indeed unique but also that he is essentially related to others. Woman, having discovered that she is essentially related to man, must discover that she is also essentially related to the world. This is her coming of age as an adult, this is, in the process of her development, the beginning of her longed-for 'promotion,' but seen in its proper perspective. What woman is for man in the building of the home, she must also be for society in the building of the world.

The life of woman is one of openness: openness to man, to her child, to her home and family. She must be in the world, for it is she whose thoughts are absorbed with the life of man, it is she who listens to his deepest aspirations, those beyond mere physical need. The life of woman is one of giving and one of redeeming, she gives herself to man, she gives herself to her child, and her love is quite prepared for every sacrifice which may be necessary to redeem and save those who have stumbled and fallen. She must bear witness to the efficacy of self-giving and redemptive love in a world of technological efficiency, a world of injustice and cruelty. Woman was made to bear life. She bears within herself the gift of her husband, she bears her child, she can find fulfilment only in maternity. In the contemporary world, the world in which the material reigns, woman is called upon to give birth to the human element.

Woman must continually remind man in his pride that he is incomplete. She must remind man in his egoism that he must transcend himself. She must remind the world that it compromises its noblest aspirations when it makes light of the human person and that the spirit of man can not bring the world to completion without the help of God. Modern man desperately needs woman, her insights, her tenderness, her graciousness, her sense of personal values, her concern for detail, her ability to adapt herself . . . , so that our institutions, our laws, our way of life may be made responsive to the values of the person, and so that a world may come into being in which men can achieve their supernatural destiny.

The 'promotion' of woman will occur when she becomes fully aware of her responsibility in regard to the building of the world and when she is willing to be present in the world and to play her proper role in it at every level, economic, political, social, in short, from the small cell of the family to the complex organizations of society. Then will the world find completion, the world which at the beginning God entrusted to both man and woman.

Vocation of the Single Woman

How many single women there are today who are convinced that their lives are wasted.[1] *There are some who hide their bitterness only with difficulty and who in spite of themselves try to take out their frustration on others. Some devote all their time to the pursuit of pleasure in hopes of filling their emotional void and of providing for themselves a comfortable life at any cost. Others, having resigned themselves to their fate, 'try to*

*make the best of it'; they no longer trouble about it,
but busy themselves with their work. If Christians, they seek
peace of mind through a careful observance of the moral
law or satisfaction for their emotions through an uninspired
life of devotions. As we come to a deeper appreciation of
their disappointment, their rebellion, their struggle, their
suffering, we must sympathetically make them understand
how gravely mistaken they are. The celibate life is not
a waste, rather it is an invitation to complete self-
fulfilment, but in a way different from that of family life.
Only self-love is sterile.*

Perhaps you have just never met the *right* man. Peter was
in love with you, but his family refused to let you see one
another any longer because you didn't have the money to
get married. You rejected John because he wasn't the
knight in shining armour you had in mind. Paul was killed
in an accident. Taken up with family obligations or with
your work you have remained single. As the years go by
solitude gradually begins to enfold you like the darkness of
night. You see happily married couples, you see the children
of your friends . . . and you experience the pain of loneliness. Who are you? To your family, you are still a child:
'Did you close the door?' 'Your light is still on.' 'There is a
letter for you, it's from so-and-so.' 'You shouldn't wear
your hair like that!' To your acquaintances, you're an *old
maid:* ' It's too bad she was never able to settle down.' In
your own eyes, all too often, you're simply a failure. It is
unquestionably true that a single person is in some sense
incomplete: 'It is not good for man to be alone.'[2] Because
each person is created in the image of God he is thereby
called to a communal life, a life of oneness with another or
others. He is called to a creative life, one rooted in love.

Every man must marry and every man must bring new life into the world but there are many levels at which this life of community and fatherhood (or motherhood) can be realized.

The physical union of man and woman in marriage ('They shall be two in one flesh'[3]) is not the only union possible in life. There is the possibility of a spiritual union with all men, which is born of love and a desire to be of service, and even the possibility of a supernatural union with the whole of mankind in Christ which is born of a charity which embraces all men. Physical fruitfulness is not the only possibility open to man for he can also be fruitful at the spiritual level; in fact he can be fruitful even at the supernatural level, in Christ. Your life is not wasted because you find it necessary to seek union and fruitfulness at a higher level. As a result you are called to a personal perfection which is more difficult to attain but which is at the same time more profound and more fruitful.

The personal vocation of each is without doubt for that particular individual the most sanctifying. But considered in itself a virginity which is willingly accepted, or even more so a virginity which is freely offered, is a state of life superior to that of marriage,[4] for the body of man is a limitation. Only the spirit opens onto the infinite. He alone is sterile who lives without love, for love is always the bearer and creator of life. Your state in life assumes its importance from the love with which you live it. Love and you will bring new life into the world.

No one can fully realize all the possibilities of his particular vocation unless that vocation is generously accepted for what it is. Every vocation involves a conscious and free reply to the call made by God. Perhaps the pressure of circumstances has forced you into a life of celibacy, a vocation which you would not have chosen had you been offered an alternative. As long as you merely endure your vocation you will not be living it. If you would experience the joy which follows upon the opening out of your personality, a life of fruitfulness, you have to accept your vocation by freely and faithfully living it to the full.

Perhaps for a long time now you have been uncertain about your vocation and this has caused you a great deal of mental anguish. Should I continue to hope for the joys of family life or should I build my life around my present state of celibacy? No life is simply a ' given' fact; your particular talents and the circumstances of your life, willed as they are by God, indicate the direction your life is to take. We are sometimes asked to remain almost wholly in the dark as we try to determine what the Lord in his love has planned for us. Purity of heart and detachment will greatly help you to read the circumstances of your life as signs indicating the will of God in your regard. Live your present life to the full, leaving yourself open to God's plans for you in the future.

Just because two young people enjoy each other's company doesn't necessarily mean that they should get married. Feelings of affection are only one sign among many. Just because you genuinely desire to get married doesn't necessarily mean that you are called to the married life; the element of attraction is only one among many in determining vocation. Beware of your imagination in this regard. In the world of dreams it seems an easy matter to establish a home and to rear children. In the world of reality, your sacrifices will seem to you superhuman because you will be forced to renounce your dreams. The world of reality is sure to contradict your world of dreams.

Once you go beyond safe, reassuring appearances it is

impossible to determine the true scope of your fruitfulness in the world. You do not have to be any less adult for leading a celibate life, for maturity implies personal autonomy, not a marriage licence. You haven't the right, as the slave of a badly understood obligation, to limit your life to a rhythm established by ageing parents. You have to learn to break binding ties. Are you afraid to cause any suffering? Are you afraid of misunderstanding, tears, harsh words? Are you using filial affection and devotion as a mere pretext, thus denying your parents the maturity to which they have a right? In spite of all appearances to the contrary, you are forcing them to halt on their own personal journey to maturity. You do not love them sufficiently.[5] Parents do not bring children into the world and rear them for themselves but for others and for God (whatever their state in life may be). Until parents have completely surrendered their children they have not as yet fulfilled their vocation as parents. If they try to hold their children back, be it ever so slightly, from others (their husband, wife, children, profession, vocation, the human family, or God) they have failed in their vocation. They do not love their children sufficiently.

It is only with difficulty that you will be able to attain a genuine autonomy if you do not strive to win a relative degree of independence from your parents. If circumstances allow, take an apartment for yourself, even if it's not a very elegant one. If this does not prove feasible, at least make sure that you have your own room.[6]

Have you really accepted your single state, have you really placed yourself in circumstances conducive to your personal development, have you really done anything about making your life a full and fruitful one if you stay locked up in your ivory tower, if you merely vegetate throughout your life, if you refuse to give yourself to the world for the service of your brothers? To make a success of the single life you have to sublimate your drives and needs, but sublimation does not imply a flight into a dream world, or an escape from reality into some vague idealism, or the search for compensating satisfaction. Rather it means accepting your drives for what they really are even though they may at times prove a source of worry to you: direct them, draw them together into a unity, and consciously orientate them with a view to a higher, fuller life.

The single girl does not have to stifle her affective life. On the contrary, she must develop it, for her love must transcend narrow parochial confines and reach out to embrace the very ends of the earth. Don't spend all your time with just one friend; your emotional life will be the poorer for it. Don't limit your circle of friends just to other single girls, for it will restrict your possibilities for growth. Don't visit one family exclusively; it could be dangerous, because the spirit may be willing, but the flesh is still weak. Don't attach yourself to some particular priest; it will prove mutually disadvantageous. Rather welcome one and all into your life, beginning with those who are nearest you: that ageing neighbour, that widow who can't find work, those engaged friends who are unable to get an apartment, that adolescent who's trying desperately to find himself. . . .

Open wide the doors of your heart to the problems of the world; offer your services without apprehension to your neighbour, your fellow workers, to some public service organization. . . . Don't run away from responsibility; you have an obligation to take an active concern in the destiny of your brothers. If you are denied the joys of the family, let this be an incentive to serve all men. Then if you've had doubts about your own ability to cope with life, you'll take on a new air of self-confidence. If you've found your life too confining, you will have a new opportunity for greater self-expression. If solitude has caused you a great deal of suffering, a network of contacts with the world—including of course contacts with the opposite sex—will help you to broaden and liberate your personality. If your faith has grown somewhat anaemic, it will assume a new vigour, one worthy of an adult. The Lord has need of the single woman, a woman who places herself at his service so that she can be the mother of the human dimension in an inhuman world.[7]

Don't seek refuge in a sentimental religiosity, for your love of God would then be little more than the pursuit of personal satisfaction.[8]

Rather open your personality to God and to your brothers; then you will know the joy of self-giving. This gift of self, however, demands a spirit of detachment, of concern for others, and of interior peace. Amidst the problems and difficulties to be found in every human life let yourself be guided by the Holy Spirit. If you are able to recognize your own weakness, to remain attentive to God through poverty of spirit, and to accept his invitations with generosity, he will indicate to you the path to be followed amidst the varied circumstances of your life. After you have travelled far down the road of life, turn and look back over the route you have taken. Then you will understand why God chose you out in a special way and, without the slightest regret, you will be able to say thank you.

Adolescence: Preparation for Love

Man draws our interest at each stage of his development,
but the adolescent engages our attention in a special way.
He is at a period of life fraught as much with possibilities
as with dangers; his personality is just beginning to open
out on the world, yearning for the fulfilment which
a new family life alone can bring. One of the most
important aspects of the interior drama of the adolescent is
precisely this hunger for love which he is not yet able to satisfy.
This need he experiences is a pressing invitation to prepare
himself for the future; during this period of waiting he is
to learn something of the meaning of love. We must take the
time to illumine the way for these young men and women.
Perhaps we should do as much for those to whose care
they are now entrusted so that they may be able to guide
them in their search instead of judging " the present generation"
out of hand.

The young boy or girl has not been destined by God to a
life of solitude and loneliness. In his eternal plan, man and
woman are meant to meet and to form a lasting union:
'It is not good for man to be alone.' [1] You are, then, called
to a communal life, but no merely transient experience of
community—even friendship—can sound the depth of
marital union. Marriage involves the free gift of one human
person to another, the one offers himself unreservedly so
that the other may open the doors of her interior personality
to receive the gift of the beloved and may in this way be
fulfilled. Love at its deepest level is a mystery of union.

The physical union between husband and wife is a source of stability for each and an opportunity for self-liberation; through their psychological union husband and wife are mutually fulfilled, completed, and perfected. So efficacious is this mutual gift of self that it has the power to confer grace on both. In virtue of their complete acceptance of one another in the marriage ceremony the engaged couple administer the sacrament of matrimony to themselves, the priest acting simply as an official witness. Again, the differences between the two sexes are not only physical in character but psychological as well, involving the whole of the personality. It is therefore the whole man who seeks a complement in the other.

Hunger and thirst are healthy drives unless you eat and drink solely for your own pleasure and in excess of what is reasonable. We must eat to live, not live to eat. Physical desire is a healthy drive unless you use your creative possibilities simply for your own pleasure and outside the plan of God. You want to achieve self-completion at every level of your life: physical, affective, and intellectual. The temptations which you experience are *at their inception* simply instinctive attempts to mould you into a unified whole and thus fulfil your personality. A child who is just beginning to walk leans on everything he can find to help himself along. We know that a man whose lips are parched will waste no time in trying to get some water to slake his thirst. The adolescent because of his emotional dissatisfaction bends all his energy to *getting* what he feels to be lacking. It is only natural that his first efforts should be centred on getting rather than giving. It takes a long time and a good deal of effort for him to pass from self-seeking to self-forgetfulness.

To love does not mean to seize the other for your own

fulfilment but rather to give yourself to the other for his or her own fulfilment. You are ready for the experience of genuine love when your need, and especially your desire to give, is more compelling than your need and your desire to get. The athlete who refuses to train and throws himself into active competition prematurely will soon enough be forced to quit the game. The painter or musician who refuses to accept the discipline necessary for perfecting his art is condemned to mediocrity. The adolescent who is in a hurry to satisfy his hunger for love and refuses to take the time necessary to prepare himself for genuine love, is seriously deceiving himself, and his abortive attempts to satisfy his craving are doomed to failure, since he is compromising the depth and integrity of his future personal unity. It requires several years to become a doctor or an engineer, why are we afraid to admit then that it takes a long time to prepare ourselves for love?

If you want a rush job on your house you can build without a foundation, you can nail the roof on before the walls are completely up, you can paint over wet plaster, and then you can proceed to make fun of your friends who still have a lot of work left to do in order to finish a home which they want to be well-built, sturdy, and attractive. Your dwarfish little structure will be sent sprawling by the first storm that comes up. If you are willing to accept— merely for your own gratification—every easy opportunity for love that comes along, you may perhaps experience the ephemeral illusion of rapid development— like nailing the roof on before the walls are completely up or putting a bright coat of paint over wet plaster—but you are preparing a family life without a stable foundation, and it will soon come tumbling down.

The physical desires which the adolescent feels are not

motivated by love; they are the excitement of a young
boy in the presence of femininity (not the other person
herself) or of a young girl in the presence of masculinity
(not the other person himself); it is the mysterious inner
movement of every being which discovers, indistinctly at
first then more and more clearly, what it requires for self-
fulfilment. Anyone who bases his marriage on mere
infatuation is building a family life upon a foundation of
shifting sand.[2]

The adolescent is a child who is in the process of receiving from the hands of God, through the intermediary
of his parents, personal care of and responsibility for his
body, his affections, and his mind. By developing these and
bringing them under his personal control he will become
an adult. Then he will be able to offer himself completely
and faithfully to another person so that he may fulfil that
other and receive his or her gift of self in return. Love in the
context of a family demands the gift of your intelligence,
your affections, your body, in a word, the gift of yourself.
If, as an adolescent, you say to a girl, I love you: either you
are mistaken and it is a serious mistake; or you are lying
and that is a detestable abuse of someone else's confidence
in your word. For when you say: I love you, you are in
fact saying: I am offering you the gift of myself, and *in
order to give yourself, you must have possession of yourself.* Do
you already, at your age, possess yourself?

There is certainly nothing wrong with friendships
between boys and girls; the trouble starts when they try to
play at the game of love, and love is no plaything. If you
find that you are attracted to another person because you
see in her depth of intelligence, or because she is physically
attractive, don't reach out to lay hold of the other. Rather
make use of this new drive welling up within you to

prepare yourself quietly for the gift of yourself and the acceptance of the gift of the other. Adolescence, physical, emotional, and intellectual, is a sign from God that this is the time of preparation, the time for you to prepare yourself for union with another person.

Training yourself for love doesn't necessitate a long string of conquests. It means learning to respect yourself and others so that you will be able to respect the body and person of another. It means enriching your own personality so that you will be able to enrich another. It means conquering yourself in order to give yourself to another. It means forgetting yourself, so that you won't seize the other like an animal but will offer yourself as a person. It means opening yourself to others, accepting them for what they are, trying to understand them, experiencing the give-and-take of friendship, in order that you may be able to welcome another into your life. It means becoming one with God so that in God you may be able to become one with another person. If you want to experience genuine love, learn the ways of love now by loving all men, your brothers.

Man and Technology

Modern man is being offered today the possibility of possessing a spiralling array of material goods. In this possibility consists the drama of modern man. Forgetful of the primacy of being over having, he tends to attribute

*ultimate value to the latter. The ease with which he can get
what he wants has in the contemporary world joined
forces with man's insatiable hunger for enjoyment. Even
though this facility is still greatly restricted for many
peoples of the world, they must remain vigilant lest they
be caught up in the maelstrom of unbridled desire.
Blinded by his own self-deception, man easily forgets that
his real dignity does not depend upon the quantity of his
material possessions but upon the quality of his interior life,
a life which opens onto the infinite. And so man stops
evolving spiritually, content if his castle in the sand
doesn't come tumbling down about his ears.*

You want to be just a little more important, you want to
wield just a little more power and so the whole of your life,
you scrape, and work, and struggle to get what you want.
If you have a tricycle, you want a bicycle; if you have a
bike, you want a car; if you have a hundred horsepower
model, you want two. Your material needs become increasingly demanding the more you give in to them. To
get the things you want you need money. If you're making
fifteen pounds a week you think that you can't possibly
get ahead unless you have twenty-five coming in. Once
you have twenty-five you set your sights on thirty-five.
And if you had fifty or a hundred it wouldn't be quite
enough, because you would have a certain standard of
living to maintain and after all you have to look to the
future. . . .[1]

You are not alone in your aspirations; the modern world
is in complete agreement with you. The heroes of the
modern world are the wealthy, the influential, the famous.
In the modern world, everything is evaluated in terms of
productivity whether it be a political system, a philosophy

of life, or even a human being. If you pride yourself on being an intellectual, you still think in terms of quantity rather than quality, of the amount crammed in rather than your capacity for genuine thought. You stuff your mind with the images and ideas presently in vogue, and you rubber stamp today's current opinions. Magazines, digests, and documentaries give you the impression of being quite well informed. It is right that you should want to grow, but unfortunately you are seriously deceived about the means to be taken to do so. You make a little stool for yourself and then stand on it so that you'll look taller. Then you add a few inches to it to give yourself the impression that you've grown. The real dignity of man does not depend on what he does but rather what he is. What difference does it make how tall your stool is, for it's not your material possessions that give you stature but the depth of your spiritual life which reaches out to embrace the infinity of God.

The child who wants to play will find only boredom in endless piles of toys. The real lover of music will find no enjoyment in a collection of instruments which no one plays. The person who sincerely desires to experience genuine love will not be satisfied by mere sentimentality, no matter how often it is offered. Man, who is being pointed towards the infinite at the very profoundest level of his personality, can not fill the void by piling up quantities of material goods. The greater your need to skyrocket your standard of living in order to be happy, the greater the risk you run of being continually dissatisfied and unhappy. A man who is bent on accumulating material goods and struggles to get all he can for his own enjoyment will end up finding himself totally incapable of envisioning any other goal in life. What a truly tragic conclusion to a life's work! He made an error in judgment at the crossroads of life; now he no longer realizes that there even exists another road to happiness. If someone takes the trouble to tell him that there is, he refuses to believe it.

When he becomes the slave of material goods, everything else in man's life loses perspective: the State becomes little more than a police agency necessary for maintaining order so that production and distribution can be carried on efficiently; morality merely insures that everyone will be able to accumulate all the wealth he wants; religion becomes a guarantee for self-satisfaction; alms-giving quiets the stirrings of conscience. In the eyes of your associates you may well appear to be a 'good man'; in point of fact, however, not only do you stop developing spiritually but your horizon begins to shrink and you become exceedingly petty and narrow-minded. The possession of an abundance of material goods doesn't necessarily add anything to your personality. Having what you want makes you appear well off but it doesn't actually make you *be* so.

The whole of human history bears witness to this continual confusion over what really constitutes the dignity of man. Only when men have given up the idea of building 'a city and a tower, the top whereof may reach to heaven,' [2] can they possibly hope to attain the infinite. Man first has to free himself from the tyranny of material possessions, and he can do this only if he adopts a new attitude to the material. He has to be converted.

At present you spend most of your time trying to get '*something*.' No matter what it costs, reserve a little time for becoming '*someone*': stop for a few moments to take a good look at your life, to appreciate the beautiful things in life, to learn to love freely, and to pray. But you protest: 'I'm not working for myself but for my children. I don't want them to have to go through what I had to.' If, in planning for 'their future,' you can't see past their material well-being, you are being rather shortsighted. To bring up a son doesn't just mean to give him enough to eat, but to give him what he needs to be a man as well. If you really want to provide for their future, make them into men. If you do, you needn't worry because they'll be able to satisfy their material needs in order to remain the men they are and to advance even further along the road of human fulfilment. Material wealth and power are not evil in themselves; it is only when they are considered the indispensable condition of human worth that they corrupt.

Whether you are rich or not is actually of small importance; what does matter is that you enjoy complete liberty of spirit in regard to wealth. St Paul writes to the Corinthians: 'Let those who buy live as if they possessed nothing, and let those who make use of this world live as if they did not make use of it.' [3] You don't have to possess an abundance of material goods to be crippled by them and prevented from developing fully. They will stifle your interior life if you value them more than the riches of the spirit. [4] It would be better for you to go hungry for a while rather than to allow the life of the spirit to become the victim of a creeping paralysis which ultimately makes the interior life an impossibility.

Just because you may happen to be poor doesn't necessarily mean that you are not the slave of material possessions: by dreaming about them, by envying those who do have them, by struggling to get them (not because of a hunger for justice and a love of others but because of a desire to enjoy them for yourself) you reveal your *attachment* to these things. Attachment to material goods can be just as harmful to the spiritual development of the poor as the rich. To insure against this attachment to material goods, try giving some of them away from time to time. If it causes you a twinge of regret, do it again, because that's an indication that your possessions are getting the better of you. You will end up by identifying them with *yourself*. The more detached you are from the goods of this world, the freer you will be to achieve genuine fulfilment. Jesus Christ has told us that no one can serve two masters at the same time; we must choose between God and Mammon. If you really want to become someone, then make your choice for God. Your poor little stool may offer you a few inches, but God offers infinity.

The Divine Vocation
of Man

*At the profoundest level of his personality each man is
haunted by the desire for perfection. This desire is infinite
in intent but its realization is hedged in on all sides by
untold difficulties. Even were it not necessary to take the
fact of sin into account and even if man could then build
a genuinely human life by ordering and directing his
natural drives, he would still remain dissatisfied.
In this way is the divine vocation of man revealed.
The Father wills to make sons of his creatures. Only grace
can bring man to authentic fulfilment, for only grace
can transform him completely in Christ.*

Do you know what causes you the most suffering? Your dissatisfaction, your unrest, your unresolved conflicts between what you want and what you actually have, what you would like to be and what you are, your hunger to know the mystery that is yourself and the mystery that is the world, your impatience for complete happiness, the countless little sufferings that continually invade your life, your longing for an authentic moral life and the evil you find within yourself and all about you, your thirst for love and your fruitless attempts to satisfy this thirst, the inadequacy of human love. . . . In a word, what causes you the most suffering is your failure to achieve fulfilment, your incompleteness. Don't imagine for a moment that your deepest aspirations can be satisfied by something outside yourself, for only the interior Master is able to fulfil your deepest needs and desires.[1]

Do you know what you most desire? The infinite. Infinite beauty, infinite purity, infinite holiness, infinite peace, infinite truth, infinite love, infinite life. . . . and at the same time you realize that the infinite exceeds your grasp, it exceeds the grasp of every man, for the infinite is the God who made heaven and earth. Your manifold desires for the infinite are resolvable into but one: the desire for Jesus Christ, for Jesus Christ *is* purity, truth, love, life. . . . This desire for self-completion and personal integrity is the gift of God. It is his love which has thus chosen you out: '. . . the Father of our Lord Jesus Christ has blessed us from on high *with every spiritual blessing in Christ, choosing us out before the creation of the world.* . . . In his love he predestined us to be *his adopted sons in Jesus Christ.* . . .'[2] From the very beginning God has thought of you not simply as a creature but a creature made divine. Don't rest content with being simply a son of man when

Christ offers you the possibility of becoming a son of God. Christianity is not a mere collection of religious ceremonies, or a code of laws, or a system of beliefs; rather it is in reality a life. Christianity is meant to be lived, not merely practised.

Although the human spirit opens onto the infinite, it is at the same time a limitation, for of itself it can never attain the infinite. If you would achieve total fulfilment, you must enter into the plan of the Father as revealed in his Son, Jesus Christ; you must be re-born in him; you must, in a word, put on Jesus Christ. The sacrament of baptism provides the means by which you are initiated into this new life; through it you enter into the mystery of the life and death of Jesus Christ. It is in him, the first-born of many brethren, that you become a son of God; it is in him, the brother of all, that you become a brother to all men.

Evil has taken such a hold over your life that you are unable to vanquish it by yourself and you know it. Jesus Christ has taken upon his own shoulders the burden of your guilt and has redeemed you from it. But you must receive this Redeemer into your life, for you can only be saved from the encompassing forces of evil by Jesus Christ, your Saviour.[3] A vine and its branches constitute a single unity as do the head and members of the body. United to Jesus Christ through the life of grace you become one with him and his Mystical Body. A river dries up if it is cut off from its source and with the setting of the sun the light disappears. You can not live your life to the full if you reject Jesus Christ. The life of the risen Saviour must become your life—this is precisely what is meant by the expression: the life of grace.

The life of Jesus Christ takes hold of your intelligence through faith. You want to understand the mystery that is yourself and the mystery that is the world; in the light of faith you can see yourself and the world as God sees them. The life of Christ takes hold of your emotions, your will, and your affections through charity; you want a love without any limitations, now you can love with the heart of God. The life of Christ takes hold of your activity and all your desires through hope; you want to make a success of your life; now you can receive into your life the very power of God. With this power comes the certainty that your triumph will be an eternal one.[4] The life of Christ takes hold of your body and sows there the seeds of immortality. You want to live your life to the full, in Christ you will live forever. If you are willing to receive Jesus Christ into your life 'at every level of your human make-up,'[5] the Holy Spirit will gradually transform the whole of your life from within.

Jesus Christ instituted the sacraments as the means of a person-to-person encounter with him, and through them he communicates his risen life. If you deprive yourself of this meeting with Christ, you are seriously endangering your ultimate fulfilment. Jesus Christ does not ask you simply to stand in awe of him, or to imitate him or even to become his friend, rather he desires that your whole life be completely transformed in him. St Paul personally experienced what it means for a man to be made divine in Christ Jesus: 'It is no longer I who live but Christ who lives in me.'[6] The work of Jesus Christ has not yet been brought to completion. It will be complete only when this new life has re-established order in the life of every man;[7] when the whole material universe becomes the servant of the new man and is thus reoriented towards God; when the Mystical Body of Christ reaches full maturity, the whole of humanity having been reunited by the spirit of love. Then the plan of the Father will have been accomplished:

'to re-establish all things in Christ, both those in the
heavens and those on earth.'[8] If you make your choice for
Jesus Christ, you must generously take part in his mission.
A Christian's life must become Christocentric, in its every
detail; the Christian is called to co-operate in the realization
of the master plan of the Father. The life of Christ in you
must transform every aspect of your life by your continual
efforts to become a 'man who stands on his feet' and to
become one with all men through an all-encompassing
love.[9] In this way you will be helping to bring the Incarnation of Jesus Christ to fulfilment throughout the whole
breadth and width of time and space. Through your
struggles and sufferings, generously accepted and freely
offered to God, you are helping to spread abroad the fruits
of the Redemption; through your love within the circle
of the family and through your work, whether it be
intellectual, manual, or artistic, you are helping to bring
God's creation to completion. In short, you are in Christ a
builder of the kingdom of God.

Your own personal fulfilment and that of the world
in which you live will never be achieved in this life. It
is 'only at the end of time' that all will be accomplished
in the risen Christ, when we will all be gathered together
to live an unending life of love patterned on that of the
Holy Trinity. In hoping to fulfil yourself completely in
this life you are setting limits to your possibilities. You
will attain to wholeness only with the resurrection of the
body and there is only one way leading to that goal:
Jesus Christ.

PART TWO

Man and His Life

Accepting Yourself as You Are

*Many find that their interior life is at a complete
standstill and that as a result they are leading lives of
'quiet desperation,' lives with little purpose and efficacy.
The reason for this is that they have never accepted
themselves as they are, with all their limitations and
all their possibilities as well.*

*What is demanded of them is a sincere candour in
regard to their real situation and a humble offering of
themselves to God. In this way they will be set free from
their inhibiting fears; in this way they will learn to be
themselves. This is, in the last analysis, the only way that
they will be able to make a success of their lives and
be of service to others.*

Perhaps you are in poor health, or you have little education,
or you find yourself handicapped, or you are unattractive,
or you lack a winning personality. . . . Or perhaps your
family has never encouraged and helped you to satisfy your
personal needs and desires. Perhaps your friends don't
understand you, or perhaps you feel that you are getting
nowhere at your work when you could be making something of yourself. . . . In short, your possibilities are limited
by your own defects and an unsympathetic environment,
and so naturally you are discouraged and ready to give up.
Take a good look at yourself: you have never really
accepted your limitations. The proof? The thought often
occurs to you: If I were in good health, I'd . . .; if others

understood me, I'd be able to . . . ; if . . . , and so your whole life is prefaced by if's. Yours is a life dominated by envy of others and by personal despair. Do you often find yourself saying: Sure, he can do it but not me. . . . If I had his brains, his education, and his personality . . . if . . . , and is there a spiteful tone and a note of rancour in your voice— directed at yourself, your environment, and life in general?

As long as you refuse to accept yourself as you are, you will never be able to build a full life for yourself because you will spend all your time wishing you had the tools that others have to build their lives without recognizing what you already have at your disposal. Your tools may be different but they can be just as good for your purposes. Don't bother yourself about having the tools others have, find out what your own are and get down to work. Don't refuse to acknowledge your limitations; that would prove disastrous. To deny their existence doesn't make them go away. If they do exist, to ignore them would be to give them the opportunity to undermine and to destroy your life. On the contrary, accept them as they are, neither exaggerating nor minimizing them.

If there is something you can change, what are you waiting for? Get busy, but with a calm perseverance. If there is something you can't change, accept it as it is. It's not a matter of 'resigning' yourself to your fate by hanging your head in despair. You have to learn to lift it up and say yes to reality. It's not a matter of letting yourself be bested by it. Bear it and offer it to God. Rest assured that God sees you and that in his eyes you are no more and no less the object of his love than those whom you presently envy. Place your cares, your sufferings, your sorrows in his hands. . . . Believe more confidently in his strength and less in your own ability to cope with your problems. To the degree that you recognize your limitations, accept them and offer them to him. You will discover that your poverty has become the very source of your wealth.

Your limitations are not simply obstacles to your success; they are also indications from God of the path your life is to take. Perhaps you are not much of a conversationalist. Is this not perhaps a sign that you should learn to be a good listener? Perhaps you are shy; rather than trying to impose yourself on others and dominate them you should make your life one of genial hospitality and graciousness. If you are not overly intelligent this may mean that your life is meant to be one of more intense activity . . . etc. . . . Recognize, accept, and offer your limitations, but do the same with your possibilities for development as well.

You have some strong points, too, and it is not a sign of humility to think that you are completely devoid of any; rather it's either sheer pretence or mere nonsense (unless, of course, it's the indication of a neurosis). To acknowledge the gifts which the Lord has bestowed upon us is not something bad. Pride enters into the picture when we are under the impression that we have merited or acquired these gifts by ourselves. The genuinely humble man fears nothing, not even himself. He is not afraid of acknowledging his accomplishments or his limitations. He is not afraid of others, nor is he afraid of his environment. His only fear is the salutary fear of the Lord which is the beginning of wisdom.

When you receive a gift from a friend, you usually open the package immediately, admire your gift, indicate your approval and thank the giver. Your heavenly Father has given you many different gifts, but all too often you do not even dare to look at them and enjoy them. You play the saint and you don't even take the trouble to be polite to the Giver. The gifts of your heavenly Father aren't solely for your own personal use. They were given to you for others and for him as well. If you have received more, more will be expected of you. And so if you have anything to fear, it's not the acknowledgment of your gifts but your failure to make use of them.

Accept yourself, but accept yourself in relation to others. Why are you afraid of your boss or your fellow workers, of anyone who is more intelligent than you, of anyone who can express himself better than you, who knows more about the subject than you? Why does he make a favourable impression on you? Why are you so shy, why are you paralyzed by your inferiority feelings? Precisely because you have not accepted yourself as you are in relation to others and you are afraid of what others will think. If you are afraid of others, remember that you will only begin to make a favourable impression on them if you accept yourself as you are, for you can never be the other, and in developing your own personality you provide a complement to the personalities of others.

Don't seek to live somebody else's life; it's just not you. The Father has given each of us a life to live. To try to live somebody else's life is like trying to wear somebody else's clothes because they look good on him. Don't worry about what others think. They will accept your limitations if you are willing to acknowledge them. They will reject you, however, if they sense that you are ashamed or afraid and that as a result you are trying to deceive them by pretending to be something that you in fact are not. Don't be afraid to say: I don't know, I haven't the ability, I don't understand. In this way you will be doing a service for others for they have need of someone who has the courage to acknowledge his limitations, for they will then find the courage to recognize and acknowledge their own.

Be yourself. Others need you just as the Lord has willed you to be. You have no right to put on a false face, to pretend you're what you're not, unless you want to rob others. Say to yourself: I am going to bring something new into this person's life, because he has never met anyone like me nor will he ever meet anyone like me, for in the mind of God I am unique and irreplaceable.

All of us are incomplete in some way. It is the union of all men who constitute the human family and it is their union in Christ which constitutes the Mystical Body. Your limitations are an invitation to union with all other men, a union rooted in love. Have but one desire: to be fully, without reservation, what God wants you to be . . . and then you will be perfect.

The Mystery of Joy

Every one of us wants to be happy. In fact, the history of the human race might well be considered as the story of a long and arduous quest for happiness. But happiness remains an elusive object. At the very moment that a man thinks he has finally found it, he is able to measure its limitations, he sees it vanishing from his grasp, and he begins anew to look toward still further distant shores where he hopes happiness may be found. Man in his blindness seeks for happiness precisely where he is unable

to find it; and so, finding himself checkmated at every turn,
at long last he gives up and decides to abandon himself to
the fleeting pleasures of the moment—or else, giving
way to despair, he concludes that happiness is little more
than an illusion. But true happiness does exist and you
can experience it.

Your whole life is dedicated to the search for happiness, but you are like the runner who wants to win the race without knowing where the goal is. Stop for a moment to seek out the right road. Your every action is ultimately aimed in the direction of happiness. It is God himself who has planted this hunger for happiness in the very depths of the human heart. You were made for happiness and this hunger which you feel is an invitation from God, an invitation echoing down the corridors of his eternity. This hunger will not go unsatisfied, for God does not plant a seed which he has no intention of harvesting. Listen to his call and welcome it as coming from God.

We have all experienced pleasure and joy in our lives. Pleasure might be defined as the happiness of the body, joy that of the soul. Don't rest content just with pleasure; it will never fully satisfy you. If you feel unhappy, it's precisely because you are being pulled apart by your hunger for pleasure, and the more you try to satisfy this hunger the more acute it becomes. Then, of course, you feel all the more unhappy. If your life is spent exclusively in the pursuit of pleasure, you are condemning yourself to endless dissatisfaction. The pleasure of the moment begins to wither almost as soon as it blossoms; our pleasures are soon swallowed up in time's relentless torrent.

Joy, on the other hand, is a reality of the spirit and shares in the spirit's immortality. Welcome it into your life and you will at the same time experience something of eternity. Your problems, trials, suffering, and death should never be allowed to extinguish the joy of the spirit. Pleasure and suffering, to be sure, are incompatible companions, but joy is able to transcend even the most trying of sufferings. It must be clearly understood from the beginning that pleasure is not something bad, so long as it is not pursued as an end in itself. Gratefully accept those pleasures which are the gift of God to help you on your way through life. But once you stop along the way to seek them out for yourself your joy will evaporate into thin air.

The road that leads to happiness takes its point of departure at your doorstep and radiates out to others, not vice versa. You're unhappy? Why? Is it because no one has taken any notice of your work, your successes, your efforts? Is it because you have something you want to say but no one will listen? Is it because you feel unloved and unappreciated? Ask God to forgive you for your melancholy, then turn your attention outwards to others. Ask about their lives, listen to them, show some genuine interest in their work, admire their good points, take note of their accomplishments . . . and these others, without ever suspecting it, will free you from your own concerns and will hold out to you the gift of joy.

Why are you out of sorts today? Perhaps you don't know why exactly. Offer the Lord your exhaustion, your frustration and all those cares which are constantly arising to disturb your peace of mind. And then smile . . . at your wife, your brother, your neighbours, your colleagues. . . . Your smile will manifest your joy, your joy which had just seemed so far away. Your joy will begin at precisely the moment that you abandon the search for your own personal happiness to seek the happiness of others.

If you find, however, that you are still bothered by your usual melancholy, stop for a moment and try to find out what's the matter. You will always discover at the deepest level of your personality traces of your own self-love. Don't give up. Offer to God what you are still trying to hold on to for yourself, and then turn from your own affairs to seek out the happiness of your neighbour.

A conflict arises within each of us from the fact that our desires are infinite, whereas our ability to realize them is strictly limited. You must also realize that you can never be fully happy without God, who alone can satisfy your infinite longing. The reason for this is that the hunger for happiness which each one of us experiences is in actuality a hunger for God. Woe to the self-satisfied who have extinguished the flame of desire for the infinite by drowning it in the shallow waters of finite pleasures. Blessed are they who still feel the gnawing bite of this hunger. Joy has to be awakened by continual giving, but this demands self-forgetfulness, and ultimately it demands a death to self. Joy is nothing less than that new life which we find in losing the old life of sin. In Christ and through him the mystery of joy is made equivalent to the mystery of the resurrection. Where do you stand right now in relation to Christ? The measure of your intimacy with him is exactly the measure of your joy. The life of God is pure joy precisely because it is pure giving. God is joy and in giving yourself to God you are giving yourself to joy.

The Weight of Worry

Each one of us finds himself tormented by worries of one kind or another and because we are in some sense infinite, we are always able to make room for still more. Many of these worries are, to put it simply, mis-directed and consequently have to be eliminated from our lives.
At times, nonetheless, our worries are quite well founded and even noble in their concern for others, but we are too weak to bear them single-handedly. Still less are we able to resolve them. Worry can paralyze, and if we would live a full life we have to give our worries to someone else to carry. But there is Someone who desires to do just that.

Perhaps you have stomach trouble, or a headache, or asthma, or ulcers, or your hair is turning white, or your face is beginning to show signs of advancing age or perhaps you're tired out and discouraged. Your life seems an endless maze of problems—I don't know where to turn, I'll never know peace of mind—and so you drag out your life, only partly alive, never knowing the taste of true joy or true peace. In large measure this is the case because you find yourself constantly disturbed by an army of worries, an army which grows in force with each passing day, an army which has been on the march for many years now in your life, an army which is determined to annihilate you, slowly perhaps but without fail.

It's not so much the difficulties that you meet with in your daily experience which threaten to overwhelm you but rather all those frustrations pent up inside you, unable to find release. Feelings of jealousy, which gnaw away at you each day, whether you frankly admit their existence or whether you conceal them behind a veil of melancholy, sulking, bitterness, or pointed silence. The rancour you feel because you don't stand out, because you're not noticed, because you're passed by; your fear of some person or of something that's about to happen or of some temptation. Your fear of not making a good impression, of failing, of not being accepted. Anger and the desire for revenge: he'll pay me back or else, I'll get him back for that, if only I'd known. . . . Feelings of doubt: I won't succeed, that's impossible, that's too difficult for me, he'll never understand me. Your regrets: if I'd only known, if I could only start all over again, I'll never get over that. Your lies, your malice, your negative attitudes, your backbiting, your calumny, your envy . . . and all the rest of like coin. This poison which each day finds its way into your conversation, your smiles, your gestures, your plans, this poison which first eats away at your own personality and then becomes a weapon against others.

Your potential for a life of love is practically infinite, but your possibilities are limited on every side by hereditary influences (which also can affect you in a positive way for the better) and by your own personal failures and inadequacies. The whole of your past history is waiting to find expression anew in your life: your useless daydreaming, your reading, your experience, your desires, your yearning for vengeance, your delight in vainglory. Don't you often find yourself drawing upon this storehouse of your past life for acts and attitudes which you should have discarded long ago?

You can see within yourself tendencies to evil which are easily discernible, which you can, as it were, pinpoint. Some others have apparently disappeared from view, buried beneath your experiences over the years. There are others which have been repressed, never to be recalled, and they really do seem dead and buried. Nothing could be further from the truth. All of your past history lives on in the present. This history is at work day and night, whether you are engaged in thought or not, whether you are conscious or not. This evil which lives on, like a cancer, has the power to undermine the health of the spirit. Impossible, you object. How could my spite, my hurt feelings of yesteryear have any bearing on my present life? What has my failure to understand others, my contempt, my indifference, all past now, what has all that to do with my life today? The disappointments I have known at various times in my life are all past history. My trials, my failings . . . all are over and done with. Let sleeping dogs lie. But don't be fooled; even though they have apparently departed and been forgotten, all these acts and attitudes of your past live on and continue to exert their influence.

Food that's gone bad in your refrigerator can poison you and your family unless you throw it out. A nail in your tyre can puncture the tube unless you pull it out. Your past worries, the important ones and the insignificant ones, can poison your whole life unless you do something about them. You should be ashamed of some of the worries which have occupied your time and you should ask forgiveness for them at the same time that you try to eliminate them. You do, however, have to concern yourself with earning your daily bread, with providing for the future, with the education of your children, with justice and peace, with your brothers, with the world in which you live and which must be redeemed.

These concerns and many more like them you encounter

each day under many forms and in many different circumstances. Should you accept these worries as an integral part of your life and learn to bear them patiently? No, because you are too weak. You have to give them into God's keeping. But then what are you personally doing? You are giving. Is that too simple? Not at all. It's extremely difficult to maintain a genuinely childlike attitude, to keep nothing back for yourself, always to give everything—even your joys—into someone else's keeping. It's extremely difficult to walk at his side, always to keep your hand securely in his, to become so small, so guileless, so lowly that you agree to let yourself be carried. Perhaps you're too 'grown-up.' When will you understand that you can't carry anything without him, not even yourself?

Cast your Care upon the Lord

Unless we learn to live care-lessly, we will be fruitlessly wasting our strength on the air. Life's difficulties besiege us from every side and even break through the outer ramparts to keep our interior life in a state of constant confusion. We can not long keep up the good fight and get the better of the forces arrayed against us unless we can spontaneously and sincerely give all our problems into the Lord's hands. It takes many long years to learn to exchange our own personal weakness, at each step of our lives,

*for the strength of God. But once we have achieved this
necessary renunciation, we will soon experience the peace
of God in our lives.*

You don't mix dirty and clean clothes together any more
than you put rotten apples in with fresh ones. You have to
banish every trace of worry (past, present, and future) from
your life if you would know true peace. Otherwise, your
worries will start to fester and spread. It's not a question of
trying to do everything in your power to forget your
worries, or to crush them, or to deny their existence. If
you do, they may disappear temporarily only to reappear
at a later date. Rather, recognize them for what they are,
try to see where they came from, and why they are
continuing to bother you. But don't engage in a useless
dialogue with them. Above all don't try to fight them.
Instead give them into the Lord's keeping.

You won't be able to free yourself from them in one
try. You will continually have to give evidence of the
sincerity of your gift. You will continually have to renew
your offering, for it will never be perfect. But if you make
up your mind not to keep back for even a moment one
single worry, and thus to give everything immediately
into the Lord's keeping, you will experience what it is to
be strong with the very strength of God. Does something
from your past life worry you? Some failing? Why? You
can't do anything now about the past. Your continual
remorse is misguided, it is only a cover-up for your spite,
your wounded vanity, your pride. Regret is born of love
but, once healed by the hand of pardon, love will set its
face resolutely towards the future. Unless you make your
failings, your remorse and your regret, things of the past,
they can effectively cripple your present life.

Perhaps it is the thought of the future which bothers you. You dread having to start a new job, or going to an interview you must face, or perhaps you dread something you have to do, or some temptation you find particularly trying. Why are you so afraid? The future isn't here yet; don't waste your strength on thin air. Give the future into the Lord's keeping, every detail of it, and live the present moment to the full. Is it the present that makes you anxious? You just can't face the problems that confront you . . .? Why? It's not the problems that count but the way you face them. If you're up against a wall, don't just keep beating your head against it. Look at it coolly and calmly, see how high it is. If it's too solid and too high and you can't get around it, accept the situation as it is. Offer it to God, offer your disappointment at not being able to deal with it. Then take another route.

Some people overload their cars, consequently cutting down their speed and ruining their motors. What about you? You can carry today's burden, the Lord will give you the grace you need. But you can't add tomorrow's burden, and the next day's as well, without courting disaster. You don't have any grace for the extra load. This time, however, you can't choose another route. You have to accept things as they are. Perhaps it's an illness, a handicap, a visitor, a job, bills to pay, the education of your children, something that has to be done, a decision that has to be made. . . . Don't immediately join issue with the problem. Take your problem as it is and offer it to the Lord without any reservations together with the anxiety that it's causing you. How am I going to do it, how am I going to get out of this spot, what path should I take? Confidently give all into the Lord's keeping: your uncertainty, your fear, your humiliation, the reactions of your acquaintances, what people are saying and what they will say.

If you have to decide on a course of action right away, wait a moment at least, or if you have the opportunity wait for a week or two and then come back to your problem and do what has to be done together with God. You'll see that your difficulty isn't quite so formidable now, for God has given you a new light and a new strength to cope with your problems. He is so much wiser, so much stronger than you!

One minute you're telling God that you've put all your trust in him and then you turn around and show him by all your worrying that you didn't mean it. If you find that you're worried and anxious all the time, that things aren't going your way, it's because you want to live your life your own way, according to a merely human pattern, staking everything on your own personal abilities alone. As soon as you surrender yourself without reserve into the hands of God, you'll discover a new strength to meet life's challenge. You can rest assured of ultimate success, although it may not be the kind of worldly success you've been dreaming of.

A child who tries to carry too much will tire himself out, will fall and get hurt. If, however, he accepts the fact that he is a child, his father will carry his load for him and even lift him up in his arms. The Lord won't force you to give him your burden of cares, your tools, your work, your life. He is always present at your side, waiting patiently and discreetly for you to give him your difficulties, but of your own accord. He's waiting for you to confide your work into his keeping. Why do you insist on keeping back so much of your work for yourself? Why do you struggle on alone and just ask God to 'help you'? Why don't you give everything to him and let him carry your load? Why don't you give him your heart and your hands so that he can make use of them in his way?

Before he died on the Cross, Christ spoke humbly to his Father: 'Father, into thy hands I commend my spirit.' Let us not forget that this same spirit was burdened with all the sins, all the suffering, all the worries of the world. Three days later, the Father called his Son to newness of life, a life of light and glory: Easter. Each night you must die to all your worries and cares, whether they be legitimate or not. In a spirit of humility, place everything in the Father's hands so that each morning he may call you from sleep to a new day, a day free from all the anxieties of yesterday. 'Into thy hands I commend my spirit: thou wilt deliver me, O Lord, thou faithful God.' [1] 'As soon as I lie down, I fall asleep in peace, since thou alone, O Lord, hast settled me in security.' [2] If you want to be free, young in spirit, joyous, peaceful, strong and successful, each day, each minute, 'Cast thy care upon the Lord and he will sustain thee.' [3]

How to be Free

When will I finally gain my freedom, the adolescent wonders. Give us bread and freedom, the working class shouts, and in order to win this freedom or to defend it against attack, the worker is quite prepared to fight and even, if need be, to die. When society wishes to punish one of its members, it simply takes away his freedom.

And yet, for the vast majority, what is freedom anyway?
Nothing more than the removal of every form of constraint,
the opportunity to do whatever one wants, wherever and
whenever he wants to. Clearly a mere caricature of genuine
freedom of spirit.
In addition to the absence of every form of physical
constraint, authentic freedom presupposes a complete
detachment from self with a view to commitment at a higher
level. In this regard, we have to win our freedom.
Human freedom is strictly finite and hence can only find
fulfilment in the supernatural order. God alone is perfectly
free. In this life, only God's most intimate friends,
those who are furthest advanced in the ways of holiness,
know the meaning of true freedom.

It would seem that freedom is the most highly treasured
of all God's gifts to man, for it has cost him most dearly:
the suffering and death of his own Son. Out of his profound
love for us and in order that we might love him in return,
God desires that man know the meaning of genuine freedom. Most think that they are really free when they can
say: I do exactly what I want to do; which means: I'm not
shackled in any way, I'm not forced to do anything I don't
want to do, I can do pretty well what I like, no one can
step on me. This may be the kind of 'freedom' a wild
animal enjoys, but it certainly is not the freedom of a man,
let alone a son of God.

Even if you were to find yourself paralyzed and con-
fined to bed for the rest of your life, even if you were to
find yourself behind prison bars, you could still be free if
you wanted to, because man's freedom is not to be
identified with mere mobility but rather is to be situated
at the deepest level of the spirit. Unless you are reduced to

a state of unconsciousness—in which circumstances you could hardly be called a free agent—nothing can take your freedom from you, because nothing can imprison the human spirit against its will. Only *you* can effectively limit your own personal freedom. If you want to be free, you have to struggle against yourself, you have to win *your* freedom.

If you stubbornly contend: it's not my fault, I'm just like that; I can't get along without it. I'm wrong but I'll never admit it. I can't get any work done, I spend all my time daydreaming, but there's nothing I can do about it. Why do I think like that?—I guess because everyone else does; I just can't take that guy. I didn't want to do it, but I finally gave in! . . . You're not free, you're a slave. A slave to self, to your past, to your circumstances, to the world. . . . You're not free until you're a man who can stand on his feet. You're not free until the spirit holds the reins over your body, your emotions, your imagination.[1]

A boat isn't free to move even if only one single rope is holding it to the bank, nor is a balloon free to fly off even if only one single cable is holding it to the ground. And you aren't free as long as you're still attached to even one single thing, or one single person, attached in such a way that you no longer have any control over yourself. Things don't attach themselves to you, rather you attach yourself to them. You give yourself up to them as their slave. The more toys you have, the more things you have to do, the more clothes you have to wear, the more records you possess, the more money you get, the harder it will be to get free because you have more opportunities to be *attached*. By detaching yourself from these things, you win your freedom.

Freedom, however, doesn't mean indifference. It is

quite normal and natural for you to find pleasure in the world in which you live, but you have to be careful that your joys, as well as your sufferings, don't unduly influence you when it's time to choose your life's work, and that they don't prevent you from going through with your decision once you've made up your mind. What good are strong and agile legs if you don't know in which direction to run? What good are building materials if you don't know what kind of a house you want to build? What good is love if you don't know anyone to give it to? What good are your triumphs over heredity, the subconscious, the unconscious, your bad habits, your constraints; what good is your self-mastery, your desire to be of service, your freedom, if you don't know how to make use of the freedom you've won? If you're not free *for* something, you're not really free, for you will find yourself the plaything of indecision, instability, and anxiety. Real freedom is the possibility you have, once you have become detached and are master of yourself, of always choosing the good and of resolutely keeping to your choice.

If you want to be genuinely free, you must become aware of God's grand design for the world he has created, of the Father's infinite care for you. And once you have won mastery over all your physical, emotional and spiritual drives, and have placed them generously at the Lord's service, you must seek to enter fully into God's plan through a love which will make you one with his Son, Jesus Christ. If you follow your instincts exclusively, you know only an animal 'freedom.' If you will give in to emotion, to imagination, to your own will, to pride, to egoism, you will know the 'freedom' of the sinner. If, however, you do the will of God, you will know the freedom of a man made like to God, the freedom of a son of

God. The level of your freedom depends upon whose will you choose to follow. Your ability to do the will of the Father is the measure of your level of freedom. Complete independence and the opportunity to satisfy all your personal inclinations, desires, and whims, are merely caricatures of real freedom and these can readily be put to flight by obedience. For real freedom comes to fulfilment in obedience to God whose will is mediated to us through the Church, our legitimate superiors, our daily obligations, and the ordinary circumstances of our lives. Genuine obedience presupposes genuine freedom, but genuine freedom is created by repeated acts of obedience.

If you are genuinely free in Christ, nothing can stop you on your way to God, for you are able to transform both legitimate and illegitimate constraints into so many means of attaining your goal. By becoming obedient even to death, Jesus Christ has won genuine freedom for you. By dying with him to sin, you will free yourself from every form of slavery and will rise with him to a new life of freedom. In baptism you received this divinely won freedom, but only in embryonic form. By means of the sacrament of penance you are allowed to regain your lost freedom. Each time you refuse to be the dupe of sin, each time you break the ties which bind you to earth, so as to belong more completely to Christ, you become more genuinely free. You will be fully free when you have wedded yourself without reserve, once and for all, to your Liberator.

How to be Beautiful

*How many men and women are absorbed by a consuming
interest in their own personal appearance! To be concerned
about such things is of course legitimate, but to be
obsessed by them is abnormal and unnatural. Generally
we are quite mistaken in our approach to bodily beauty
care, for all our efforts to beautify ourselves exteriorly
will yield only a rather mediocre return. Real beauty
originates from within and comes to birth in the spirit;
it then manifests itself as the radiance of a soul made like
to God. This is the kind of beauty that wins admirers.*

What shade of lipstick do you use? What brand of hair
shampoo do you buy? Are you beginning to bald slightly?
Have you lost some weight? What colour suits you best?
There's nothing wrong with asking these questions so
long as you don't make a fetish out of beauty care.
However, if you want to be really attractive you'll have
to look elsewhere as well. It's very nice to have a lovely
table setting but what good is it if you haven't any food
to put on it? It's very nice to own a beautiful picture frame
but what good is it if you don't have a canvas to put in it?
A chandelier is an unusual furnishing but what good is it
if it's not connected to the electricity? If God has graced
you with a nice figure and a pretty face, be grateful to him
for it; but what good is beauty of body if in truth it is only
skin-deep? Your body could be likened to a house of
which you are the landlord, but remember that you are
also responsible to God for your property. Don't just look

after the outside of your house but see to the upkeep of the inside as well, for the Lord goes beyond mere appearances. Take care of your personal appearance but do it for others so that they can find in you a reassuring air of freshness and self-confidence.

The prettier the scenery the stronger the temptation to sit down and enjoy the landscape, and as a result to forget the reason for your trip. Physical beauty is a road which is meant to lead us to the inner beauty of the soul, the inner beauty of a soul sharing in the life of God. Don't stop half-way, you'll miss the whole purpose of the trip. We all know how striking a three-dimensional picture can be; when this same picture is reduced to one dimension it seems flat and lifeless. When we eliminate the dimension of the spirit in another we eliminate at the same time the real source of his or her beauty, for beauty should be measured by the degree to which the spirit manifests itself through external appearances. We often say: he has the hands of a violent man, or of a miser, or of an artist, or of a sensitive personality. He has a cruel face, he looks like a forthright or a hypocritical type of person, he appears to be closed in upon himself or open to others, he's a kind or an unsympathetic-looking man. We are quite right in speaking in this way, for the body, the hands, the face, each reveals the inner spiritual state of the personality. To the man who knows how to read these signs they offer a visible portrait of the man within.[1]

No one can escape the extraordinary *creative* power of his thoughts, of his emotions, of his whole interior life, for the soul is the formative element of the human composite and fashions our external appearance in much the same way that artistic genius inspires the work of art and guides the movement of the hands. Whether you will or no, your exterior appearance will bear the stamp of your interior life. In the next life, our risen body will reflect in its every detail our inner beauty of spirit. The candour of the child is always winning no matter what sort of rags and tatters he may be forced to wear, but this is an easily won beauty, that of the soul fresh from the hands of God. We can not but be struck by the beauty of the old, for this is a beauty of soul which is visible even though the face be wrinkled and the hands withered.

If your only concern is mere physical beauty, it can only be that of the rose which fades on the morrow. If, however, you seek after the inner beauty of the spirit, you are laying up to yourself treasure in heaven which the thief of time can never steal from you. The worm inside the apple will one day break through the outer skin, the decay within inevitably makes its way to the outer surface. If your heart be evil, the truth will out. Your face and hands will bear witness to the corruption within. Physical beauty elicits a physical response and those who give themselves up to its lures ultimately find themselves wallowing in the despair of their discontent. The devil uses beauty for his own purposes, seducing and enslaving those who succumb and these finally abandon all hope of inner peace. The Christian life holds its beauties too and, if we make these our objective, we will come to know the meaning of inner peace and purity of heart, for we will be on the road that leads to God. What unspeakable beauty is evident in a grace-filled life. Take for example a man like Charles de Foucauld. His inner beauty of spirit would be apparent even through a face which was hopelessly deformed. Owing to a special grace, God sometimes permits that his saints bear in their flesh certain visible marks of their Master's own humanity, but the privilege of manifesting Christ is not reserved to the saints alone. If you are living the life of Christ, your look will become the look of Christ, your smile will become his smile, your face will become his face. If you want to have a pleasing appearance, stop for a minute before your mirror, five minutes before your soul, and fifteen before your God.

How not to be Busy

Ceaseless activity is one of the most ruthless idols of the modern world. We have too much to do and yet we want to be doing everything. Since we haven't enough time we rush about frantically, wear ourselves out and end up in a state of nervous collapse or of complete discouragement. We make ourselves unbearable to others because we're over-tired, and we shorten our life span with all our rushing about. We don't get everything done that we want to and what we do is only half done. We're failures and we have to do something about it. We need a bit of self-mastery, organization, and faith to straighten out our lives.

I'm completely overwhelmed with work! Don't ever say that, don't ever let yourself say that, don't even think it. If you do, you'll end up believing it and that would be disastrous. The great men of history do ten times the work that we do and in ten times less time. Why? Because they know how to organize their work. They carefully guard their tranquillity of mind or else they are able to regain it in a short time. They put themselves completely into everything they're doing. Don't write: I haven't a minute to call my own, I only have time for a line . . . I would have liked to . . . etc. Just write what you have to say, without all the blustering. You'll save a lot of time and you'll also safeguard your peace of mind. Don't say to someone who's come to visit: I can only take a moment, I'd offer you a chair, but . . . and then keep him standing there for fifteen minutes while you do something else. Have him sit down and give him ten minutes of your time, calmly and quietly. Try to give the impression that you have nothing better to do than spend this time with him. If someone asks you to go out with him, don't start out by protesting that it's absolutely impossible because you're much too busy . . . etc. . . . because you'll end up by arranging a date with him anyhow. Simply smile and say: I'd love to, and then suggest the first open date you have, even if it's not for some time.

If you've been told several times recently: Oh, I didn't dare to disturb you the other day . . . you looked so busy, watch out: that's a serious warning signal because many more have likely come and gone away without bothering to mention the fact. Chances are that they may have needed your help that day. We don't usually confide in someone who's overly busy because it's obvious that he hasn't room for us in his life: he's too busy! If you want to be a brother to one and all, leave the door open for them to enter into your life. You have plenty of time, but you spend your time wasting it. You'll never gain time by trying to do more than one thing at a time. At supper, when you pour the milk, you fill one glass at a time. In your daily affairs, you have to learn to fill each minute at a time, otherwise some minutes will overflow while others remain empty.

Constantly tell yourself: for this moment I have only

one person to deal with, and that's the one who's right in front of me; I have only one letter to write, the one I'm writing right now; I have only one thing to do, what I'm doing here and now. In this way you'll be able to work more rapidly, more efficiently, and with a lot less headaches. Sleep and relaxation are not a waste of time. Each of us has different needs in this regard. We have to know ourselves and allot exactly the time necessary for preserving our peace of mind and ability to work. Don't take less than you need or you'll wear yourself down. Don't take more than you need or you'll become a glutton for it. Have you a lot of work to do? Offer your sleep or your leisure to the Lord and be at peace. You're not wasting your time. Time is a gift of God and he will demand of us an exact accounting of our use of it. But be at peace: God is not an overbearing father, he doesn't give us a job to do without at the same time giving us the means to accomplish it. We always have time to do what God would have us do.

When you don't have enough time to get everything done, stop for a moment and pray. Then place your work before God as you do it. What you can't finish, leave, even if others become insistent and refuse to understand, for God has not given you this work to do. You never have *too much* work to do. Once you see what God wants you to do, then leave everything else aside and put yourself completely into the task at hand. God is waiting for you here at this very moment, at this very place and nowhere else.[1]

Stop for a Moment

*All too often modern man becomes the plaything of his
circumstances because he no longer has any leisure time,
or rather, he doesn't know how to provide himself with the
leisure he needs to stop for a moment and take a good look
at himself. He hasn't time to become aware of himself as a
person. Having resigned himself to his situation, modern
man no longer even dares to recollect himself because he
would have to face up to his responsibilities, and these
frighten him. Running about wildly gives him the impression
that he's still alive and useful. In point of fact he's
walking in a daze, he's out of touch with himself, and
his life has been reduced to one of mere instinct. Hence
modern man is no longer worthy of the name, he's little
more than an animal. Learning to stop for a few
moments is the first step on the road back to sanity.*

If you're always driving your car too fast, you'll soon wear
out the motor. If you're always living *under pressure,* your
physical and mental forces will soon begin to flag. Because
you're always on the run, you never *meet* anyone any more,
not even yourself, and that's disastrous. If you really want
to re-establish communication with the deeper levels of
your personality, you'll have to learn to stop for a moment.
If you eat on the run, you can't digest your food properly,
so sit down and relax. If you try to think while you're on
the run, you'll make a bad job of it, so stop and rest. Don't
wait for God to have to bring you up face-to-face with

yourself. It will be much too late, you'll no longer be worthy of such a grace.

The teacher who's discouraged with the progress his students are making feels like giving up altogether. The housewife who's neglected her work for too long soon finds that staying at home has become repulsive. The man who has lost control over himself finally gives up in despair. He walks past the door to his interior life but no longer dares to go inside. If you haven't paid your rent you'll try to avoid your landlord at all costs. If you haven't bothered to visit one of your friends for a long time, you stay away for fear of being reproached. If you're afraid of stopping for a minute, it's because you're afraid of meeting up with yourself, and if you're afraid of meeting up with yourself, it's because you no longer know yourself. You're afraid of your own self-reproaches and the demands that might be made upon you.

You haven't time to stop! Be honest with yourself, there are a few empty moments in your day. Don't hurry off to fill them with noise, or the newspaper, or a conversation, or the mere presence of someone else. While you're waiting at the hairdresser's, don't grab for the first magazine you see. Stop for a moment. You find yourself on the bus, packed in like a sardine, lulled by the noise of the anonymous crowd. Stop your day-dreaming. Lunch isn't ready yet, don't run out *just for a minute* to see a friend down the street. Stop for a moment. You have a free moment, don't put a record on. Stop.

If the swimmer raises his head out of the water, it's so that he can catch his breath. If you take your car into the petrol station it's so that you can get it filled up. If you stop it's so that you can take stock of yourself, so that you can gather your forces together, put some order into your activity and give yourself new purpose.[1] It's so that you can give the best that's in you to the task at hand. Unless you stop for a moment, you'll never have a chance to get to know yourself. Once you have come to know yourself you are already on the way to giving your best, for now the spirit is once more at work within. You will never come to full self-knowledge unless you see yourself as God sees you. You can only act effectively if you act in union with God. When you return to your interior castle make it an encounter with God as well as with yourself.

Throughout the course of your daily life make use of the opportunities offered you to take a new hold on yourself and to welcome God into your life: while you're waiting for the bus, or for your motor to warm up, or for your supper to cook, or for the milk to boil, or for your coffee to cool off, or for a free telephone booth, or for the traffic lights to change. . . . Don't *kill time*: no matter how short it is, it can be a moment of grace. The Lord is there, and he is inviting you to reflection and decision so that you can become a man in the fullest sense of the word.

Reflect, Evaluate, Decide

It is of capital importance for a man to stop for a few moments each day but it is equally important that he make use of this break *: he needs time to reflect and to make his own personal decisions. The life of modern man is one of continual movement and extroversion, and hence*

it is becoming increasingly impersonal. Conditioned
responses are tending to replace free choices. Modern man
tolerates this status quo because he is thereby dispensed
from any personal effort. Mass man has to be re-educated
and given back his sense of responsibility. By his very nature
a man, if he is to be worthy of the name, must assume
responsibility for his life. A man can do this only if he
stops for a few moments and makes use of this time
to reflect, to evaluate, and to make a decision.
The Christian can never be content to live a merely human
life; his attitude towards life must be continually scrutinized
in the light of his faith. This question will be treated
in two later chapters: 'Behold, I Make All Things New'
and 'Re-viewing Your Personal Life.' We have discussed
in separate sections what our attitude as men and what
our attitude as Christians should be in order to make it
clear how reflection and decisive activity are essential even on
the purely human plane. It should be noted, however,
that for the Christian these are not two distinct levels upon
which our life is lived: we aren't simply men at certain
times and Christians at others. From the moment of our
baptism, we must live the whole of our lives in Christ,
as men sharing in the very life of God.

You find yourself caught up in the onrush of life's movement and never find the time to get to know yourself.
You follow the movement of the herd and allow yourself
to be guided by the strong hand of circumstance without
ever struggling to make your own way. All too often you
are little more than the victim of circumstance. At your
work—I didn't want to take this job, but after all you have
to make a living somehow. In your leisure life—well you
have to escape once in a while. In your surroundings—

that's what everybody does here. In your family life—I didn't have any choice in the matter, did I? In your home life—of course I love my wife and my children but sometimes I merely put up with them . . . that's only to be expected. . . . In your moral life—I had to do it, I didn't want to seem old-fashioned. In your religious life—my father and mother brought me up this way, I don't see any reason to change now. In your personal life—you let yourself get carried away. You're the plaything of feeling, you have a mania for... ; you are driven by passion; sensuality, pride, and jealousy have the upper hand. . . . If your life is imposed upon you from without, you're not mature yet. You must assume the direction of your life yourself.

All too often, when you're not simply the victim of circumstance, you at least try to escape from real life. You refuse to accept life as it is, daydream so as to escape its harsh realities, refuse to accept your own limitations,[1] your failures (which are the limitations imposed upon you by life itself). You won't see others as they are. If you're afraid to meet the real world, if you try to adjust it to your own liking or to escape from it instead of facing up and offering your services to it, you are not yet mature. At times you are constrained to accept life on its own terms, but then you refuse to acknowledge any personal responsibility for your actions: I had to, I couldn't do otherwise, it's not my fault. If you can't shoulder the responsibility for all your actions, you may well be a child but you're certainly not an adult. You will be a mature adult when you've made up your mind to stop for a moment from time to time to look at life with complete honesty, to evaluate your real situation as it actually is and to decide freely to live your own life.

The painter regularly stops from his work and steps

back to take a look at what he's done. You must learn to stop for a minute too and to stand back to take a look at your life. Refuse to live even a moment of your life without knowing why you are, and make up your mind how you will live it. You must take hold of your own life by learning to reflect on it and to make your own decisions about it. Every aspect of your life must become in all truth *your* life. To live your own life doesn't necessarily mean that you will have to live differently from everyone else. (That's precisely what the adolescent does who tries to affirm his own individuality.) On the contrary, it will often mean living like everyone else because you see that that's the way you *should* live and because *you've* decided to live that way. Even if you have to do such and such—keep silence at school, show up for work at a certain time, follow orders from above—stop for a moment, look at your situation and assume this obligation on your own.

Everything you do because you are forced to may be the result of little more than a conditioned response. It may even indicate that you are in actuality a slave. If you personally decide what course you are going to take or if you *consciously* choose to do what has been proposed to you, or even imposed on you, you will be acting as a man. Only human acts make you mature, only human acts make a man out of you. Bring thought and personal decision to bear on those areas of your life where you see little more than instinct, training, indifference. It's fashionable, everybody's doing it: perhaps—but make up your own mind about it. You like this film because it's had good reviews. You read this book because it's a best-seller. You watch such and such a programme because everybody else does. You faithfully read the editorials in a certain paper because it dispenses you from evaluating the world situation for yourself. You read 'digests' because the selection has already been made for you. Stop for a moment, look at the situation, and make up your own mind. Food is nourishing if you chew it first. Every aspect of your life can enrich you if you personally reflect upon it and make it your own. The more slowly the water passes through the percolator, the better the coffee. Take the time to let your daily activity pass before the discerning eye of conscience and you will make a success of your life.

It is only by developing your powers of reflection and your ability to make your own decisions that you will attain to a mature personal life. If you help someone else to approach a film, an article or another person in a more intelligent way, if you help someone else to become more fully aware of the implications of some situation or of some event which affects his life, if you help him to grasp the real circumstances of his life better, you will be helping him towards maturity and at the same time leading him closer to God. For each effort a man makes to become more fully a man brings him closer to the Father who desires that man be fully conscious and fully free in his activity.

By following the path of personal reflection and decision which leads to a life of fuller awareness, you succeed in freeing yourself from a life of conditioned responses, a life lived at the level of instincts and the senses. If you succeed in becoming a mature adult, don't stop halfway but push forward towards total fulfilment—the Father invites you to live as a son of God. If you would do so, you must see your life as God sees it, you must evaluate it as he evaluates it, you must give of yourself as he wants you to. But to realize such a goal, you will have need of a light transcending the natural light of reason—you will have to re-view your life in the light of faith.

How to Concentrate

Some men can turn out in an hour as much work as others
turn out in four. Some can resolve a problem, make a
decision, overcome a difficulty in a matter of minutes,
whereas others will waver back and forth for days.
Some can explain a particular question with utmost clarity,
write a meaningful letter to a friend, make lasting contacts
with others in a few moments' time, while others will
succeed at the very same projects only imperfectly after
several hours of work. Some can prepare themselves for
prayer almost immediately, whereas others find it impossible
to recollect themselves. This is so because—in addition to
other reasons—some know how to concentrate so as to give
themselves completely to the task presently at hand, while
others are habitually distracted, incapable of ordering and
directing their undisciplined capabilities. A man will be
effective to the degree that he is able to concentrate!

Because it can capture the light and heat of the sun and
make them converge on a single point, a magnifying glass
is able to start a fire. If you know how to bring all your
forces together for battle, at the right moment and in the
right place, you do not need to have a large army to be
successful for it will suffice to mobilize them quickly and
effectively. Concentration is not basically a mode of *doing*
but above all a mode of *being*. Consequently you can easily
learn to concentrate all your energies once you have
succeeded in unifying and harmonizing your interior life.[1]
   You will first have to learn to avoid everything which

might serve to distract you. Don't overload your cupboards, your desk, your handbag, your pockets with useless superfluities. That will help you to keep from filling your mind with useless concerns. Don't do half a dozen things at the same time. Take each problem as it arises, one after the other. Deal with one task at a time; after you've finished one, move on to the next, but only if you've the intention of tackling it seriously. Don't just glance over a book or magazine, or a letter; either read a chapter, or an article, or write a reply. Otherwise put them all aside and don't waste your time. It's by parcelling out your attention on too many things at once that you become distracted and wear yourself out. Do you want a rich crop? Then be generous with the pruning fork. Do you want beautiful flowers? Sacrifice a few buds. Do you want to be effective? Learn to limit yourself. If you try to do everything, you'll end up by doing nothing well.[2]

If your hose is riddled with holes, the water will only dribble out the end. Plug up the leaks, and the water will return to full pressure again. If you spend hours daydreaming, you're leaving the real world behind. If you're talking all the time, you haven't time to think. If you're ready to do battle at the slightest provocation, you're wasting your emotional resources. You won't be able to concentrate all your efforts when the need arises. You've too many leaks. The schoolboy whose desk is covered with toys, whose pockets are loaded with sweets and whose head is filled with jokes, can't give his attention to his work. If you want to hold back for yourself alone certain joys or sufferings, certain aspirations or dreams, no matter what they are, you will find yourself being pulled in several directions at the same time and as a result you won't be able to concentrate.

You object: I can't keep from daydreaming, I can't keep my tongue still, I can't control my feelings. You are completely right. It's not a question of suppressing the movement of life but rather of making use of it when and as you should. Don't destroy anything; rather put everything in its proper place so that you can find it when the occasion arises. And how is this to be done? By giving all into the hands of God, confidently and calmly.

The movement of life which you personally experience within: your thoughts and plans, your feelings and aspirations, your instincts and emotions, your discouragement, even your temptations—this dynamic movement of life often enough breaks forth without a well-defined purpose or direction and thus your strength is wasted on thin air. If you would make use of this vital surge of energy, you will first have to give *everything* into the hands of God in a spirit of unqualified trust. If you keep nothing back for yourself, you will make a success of everything you do because God will provide you with what you need for the task at hand.

Concentration, however, doesn't imply a frantic attempt to control each and every interior movement of life so that it will be ready for use when the need arises. Actually, it means first of all emptying yourself by giving all. In order to empty yourself you will first have to relax—your body, your muscles, your overwrought nerves—and then offer all to the Father as your gift. Look calmly towards him, survey the situation in which you find yourself and then give the best that's in you to the business at hand.

Each day offer yourself to God during a few moments set aside for recollection and silence. During the day, especially when you are upset, busy, or tense, take a moment to renew your offering of love and you will then find yourself ready to continue your work and you will find yourself working more effectively. If you're always doing something you don't want to, if you find your work a trial from beginning to end, if you just keep going because you have to, your activity, your work, your life, since they are imposed upon you from the outside, will seem little better than slavery. But if you consciously and willingly assume each one of your activities, you will find a new freedom emerging in your life, you will find it easier to recollect yourself because your life is under the direction of inner freedom rather than outer necessity.

By personally assuming responsibility for each of your actions, what you are in effect saying is this: If I learn to concentrate all my efforts on what I'm doing here and now, I'll be able to do my work much more effectively, and thus I'm increasing the value of what I do. I am not alone, my efforts fit into a larger scheme in which all men have need of what I'm doing right now. In the company of all I'm helping to build a better world, I'm helping to bring the human family together, I'm helping to save this family. It's not so much what I'm doing that counts but the love with which I'm doing it. God is present here, in fact he is the one who gave me this job to do. Your former drudgery will assume a new importance, and you will be able to give your best to the task at hand instead of giving only half-hearted response to the demands of the present moment.

Man's Work in the World

Some of us are perpetual critics, others inveterate activists,
who throw ourselves into work without even knowing why.
We have not been called by God to a life of slumber,
no matter who we are. We have to work, and work hard,
at our own self-completion. We have to work too at
building the city of God at the same time that we're
working to build the city of man. There are several kinds
of activity, however. Our activity will be fully effective
only when it becomes the activity of Jesus Christ.

It's easy enough to knock down a house, but it's somewhat more difficult to build a new one in its place. It's easy enough to criticize, but it's difficult to do something constructive. If you spend all your time criticizing, you won't have any left for getting down to work. It's easy to make plans, but it's difficult to bring them to completion. A cold-water flat is worth any number of castles in the air. Hell is paved with good intentions which never saw the light of day. Because you can't accomplish very much, you don't do anything. But it's better to light one candle than to curse the darkness. Our mental and spiritual powers are like muscles—they have to be exercised. We can't just stand still; if we try to, we'll fall back. It's only by dint of striving that we make ourselves into men. Take a look at those around you. They seem to be busy about many things and yet you will soon find them depressed and discouraged because the results of their work are meagre in comparison with the effort expended. The value and importance of an action should be measured by its inner content not by the flurry of movement which may accompany it. And this inner content depends upon us. Some men can do a great deal of work in a short space of time and with little apparent effort, others take a great deal of time to do a little bit of work with obvious difficulty. This disparity is to be explained by the differing levels of inwardness to be found here.

Animal activity is situated on the instinctual level, human activity on the level of intelligence, Christian activity on the level of faith illuminating intelligence. All too often you act as an automaton, as an animal; sometimes you act according to the dictates of intelligence, as a man; rarely do you act in the light of faith, as a Christian. To introduce reflective intelligence into action is precisely to introduce the person into what you do.[1] To introduce intelligence illuminated by faith is precisely to introduce the Christian person, a son of God, into what you do.[2] You can help others as well to bring personality to bear on their work, and even Christian personality. To accomplish this you have to help them to pass gradually from the conditioned response to reflective intelligence and finally to faith-illuminating intelligence.

If you are serious about what you are doing, you will first have to accept the real world as it is. Seek to appreciate the needs of *this* world and see what you can do to help in the light of your abilities. This is the beginning of an intelligent course of action. As a Christian you must avoid every form of self-delusion. Hence, you will have to see the real world in the light of your faith or else you will grasp only one dimension of it. Through the concrete circumstances of your own life God will mediate his will to you, inviting you to undertake some work for him.

Consequently, when your activity is based upon a faith-illumined evaluation of the needs of the real world in which you live, you are conforming to the designs of God here and now. Never forget that it is impossible to act effectively as a Christian man if you have not first seen and properly evaluated things as they really are. You must bend every effort to bring the plan of God to completion once it has been indicated to you through the circumstances of your life.[3]

You want to work effectively in the world, you're impatient at your apparent lack of results, you're overwhelmed by the thought of all that remains to be done, you appreciate the needs of those around you and of the whole human family. If you really want to be effective in the world, simply allow the will of God to become your guiding beacon. In return for your weakness you will receive his strength in your life. God can work wonders through the lowly ones of this world. You are limiting your own sphere of influence by relying on your own ability alone. You must decrease if Jesus Christ is to increase and through you bring the design of his Father to completion.

The Grace of the Present Moment

All men, but especially the young, want to live their lives to the full. They are right in wanting to do so. However, they often deceive themselves in evaluating their

*success in this regard. Some are simply deluded: they
don't actually live their own lives but are little more
than victims of instinct and whim. Some are disappointed
at their showing when they recall bygone days. Others
tend to idealize the past, transforming it into a golden age.
Some are terrified by the prospect of an unknown future.
Others look forward to it as the scene of new triumphs.
All alike forget to live here and now. There's only one
way of making a success out of your life. It's to give the
best that is in you in the framework of the present moment
by personally responding to the love of the God present
here in this situation.*

It's amazing how many men remain on the periphery of
life so much of the time, finding themselves at life's end
with little to show for their efforts. Why don't you live
your life to the full? You're always projecting yourself into
the future. You have to, you say, look out for the future—
your exams, your work, your family. Then you have to
look out for the future of your children—their exams, their
work, their families. Then you have to look out for your
retirement—your pension, your insurance, your home. . . .
Tomorrow I'll be. . . . Why do you keep putting off until
tomorrow the life you have to live today? One of these
days there will be no tomorrow, and you won't have begun
to live your life at all.

Perhaps you cling to memories of the past; it assumes a
new importance in your eyes as the work of your own
hands. But that was yesterday and today you can't do a
thing about it. You find living in the future to your liking
because you can shape it to suit your fancy. But it isn't here
yet and you're merely wasting your time.

The present is of such short duration that you don't take

much notice of it, and yet it alone counts because it alone is in your hands. In fact, the whole of your life is simply a succession of present moments.

You think you can see ahead of you a future of happiness, joy, love, and communion with God. It's only a mirage. You forget that God is right by your side, precisely where you are right now, and that all is in his hands and that his invitation is dated the present moment. Don't spend your life chasing after the shadow of God when he's already right beside you.

The restless man drags his past along behind him trying to lay hold on the future at the same time that he's 'living' in the present. The busy man will try to live several moments at once. This poor fellow destroys them all in his confusion. If you want to make a success of your life, leave the past in the hands of God, let him take care of the future as well, and give all your attention to the business of the present. When a stitch is dropped in knitting it causes a hole, for even though one stitch seems of small consequence it is nonetheless indispensable. Don't neglect a single moment of your life; each is infinitely important in weaving the seamless robe of your life.

The present moment is delicate; handle it with care. It provides only a narrow passage; there's no room for worry. It passes quickly, and so it won't tire you out. It is a moment pregnant with possibility, but you have to give it direction and meaning. It alone possesses reality and it alone provides an arena for action. Its opportunities are limitless, for in it we meet the God of love. Don't shoulder the burden of the past, refuse to give any consideration to the future simply out of fear: that's the prompting of cowardice. Don't brood over the past, refuse to be frightened by the prospect of the future, confidently abandon yourself to God: that's the prompting of love. God is awaiting you in the present moment, but if you try to take up permanent residence there, like a rock in the midst of the onrushing current, you will be left behind by the light and strength of God's grace.

In the whole vast expanse of human history there is only one point of contact with the Lord of this history: the present moment. It is through the door of the present moment that God enters into your life, and it is through you that he enters into the life of the world. But God will not step through that door unless you open it to him. Each moment is an annunciation in your life, but you can only respond to God's call if you're there to hear it. When you respond to the call the Son is once more made flesh, this time in you. When you respond to his call as manifested in the work at hand, you allow the Father to further the work of creation which is carried on in the Son. If you respond to his call by giving your all within the context of the present moment you are allowing the Son to carry out his work of redemption in the world.

The most important and most efficacious commitment of yourself that you can make is the commitment you make here and now in the present moment by leaving to God both the past and the future and placing yourself totally at his disposal. If you are faithful to this commitment you will live your life to the full and you will make a complete success of your life in the world.

PART THREE

Man and Others

Who is the Other?

The other—whomever you meet on the road of life, the man who lives next door, who works with you, who knows, as do you, the meaning of joy and of sorrow, the fellow whom you can't stand, the one you never speak to because you never bother to look at him on the street, the one you never think of because you've never seen him.

The other—the one to whom you must unite yourself in love to become fully a man by being a brother to all; the one to whom you must unite yourself in love if you would make a success of your life and join in the movement of universal salvation won in Jesus Christ.

The other—the one with whom you co-operate in striving to bring the work of creation to fulfilment. The other—the one before whom you will one day be judged. The other—the one who helps you to mature. The other—a gift of love from Christ. The other—one sent from the Father, a request for love from Christ. The other—one through whom God manifests himself, through whom God speaks to you, through whom God enriches your life, through whom God is able to measure our love for him. The other—your daily bread, your daily Eucharist.

The other's name? John, Peter, Mary, Mr Smith, Mrs Jones. He lives in the same house with you, works in the same office, rides the same bus, sits next to you at the show. The other's name? Jesus Christ. Jesus lives in the same house with you, works in the same office, rides the same bus, sits next to you at the show . . . the other! . . .

How to make Contact with Others

*Today we are witnesses to an almost universal urge—both
on the part of individuals and of nations—to establish
contact with others. The ambition of many in our society
today is to make contacts with such and such a person,
social group, or even country. Some hold this to be an
absolute necessity, others a duty. We believe that it is both.
It's a necessity because no man is an island sufficient unto
himself: it is little more than a cliché to speak of our
"shrinking world" or to maintain that the interests of all
men—regardless of distances—are bound up together.
It is a duty because man can not attain self-fulfilment
unless he becomes one with all men. It is an even more
pressing duty when we consider that all men have been
redeemed by Jesus Christ and have become in him sons of
the very same Father, and hence are brothers. To the
degree that modern methods of transportation and
communication bring men closer together they must learn to
increase their contact and also to make them more
meaningful. Is it, however, quite so simple to establish
contact with the other?*

Just because they are glad-handers and back-slappers, just
because they have a number of drinking companions and
business associates, some men are under the impression
that they have made all sorts of contacts and consequently
have a large circle of friends. They are terribly mistaken
unfortunately—a man can be quite alone in the midst of a

crowd of so-called 'friends,' unless he is willing to *see* them as they are and welcome them into his life.

You have been waiting for the bus for some time now. Then it passes you by—all filled up. You get annoyed: it's always like that on this route. In somewhat the same way there are certain persons who are always all filled up. They go right on past every stop; they have neither time nor space for those who are waiting to get on. They're too filled up with themselves. Don't you often find that you pass by others too quickly because you're all filled up? Yet no one else will stop at this particular place and at this particular time. Only you can pick up this other person here and now.

If you really want to establish contact with another, you first have to learn to *see* the other. To *see* the other, you have to make your way through life a bit more slowly, you have to take the trouble to stop for a moment, you have to be genuinely interested—in *his* work, *his* family, *his* recreation, *his* home, *his* likes, *his* aspirations, *his* difficulties, *his* struggles . . . you must sincerely desire to know him so that you can come to understand and to love him.

To make contact, *seeing* alone will not be enough. You will also have to welcome the other into your life. It can be quite as discouraging to find no room in the inn in the life of your neighbour as to be without a roof over your head. You have to see to it that there is always room in your inn, that the door is always open. Let there be no need for a 'Beware of the Dog' sign in front of your home, whether that dog be your temperament, your pride, your egoism, your jealousy, your sarcasm, your gruffness, your tactlessness. . . . Never let the other draw back with this reproach: He didn't care . . . or I was afraid that he'd throw me out . . . or that he'd make fun of me . . . or that he wouldn't understand. . . . Don't hold back so that the other becomes hesitant; welcome him immediately into your life, if only by means of a handshake or a smile if you haven't the time to have him sit down. A moment of *complete* attentiveness is quite sufficient to welcome the other. Don't let your furniture block his entry—there should be plenty of room. Don't try to impose your likes, your ideas, your point of view. If you offer the other anything let it be done with a generosity that expects nothing in return. Don't force a lease upon the other, let him come and go as he wills without having to commit himself.

One day will Christ say to you: Thank you for having room in the inn of your life—or rather—Be gone, I found not even a stone upon which to rest my head when I asked you. If you welcome the other into your life, it's so that he can rest. When you're at the railway station you look for a porter to carry your bags—be just that for others. Their bags are too heavy and too cluttered with super-fluities; let them put them down for a moment. Perhaps when they leave you they will find their load a little lighter and easier to carry. You don't make contact with everyone with whom you happen to rub elbows, because genuine contact requires something more than mere physical proximity, it involves a mysterious *encounter* between two persons.

A man's real worth is to be measured, among other things, by his ability to make genuine contact with others, but this ability is not essentially the sum of mere externals: amiability, joviality, the right word, etc. Nor is it only the result of spiritual endowments: feeling, composure, attentiveness, etc. Naturally, all these things help, but they are only prerequisites for authentic encounter. In the last analysis, the ability to make contact is to be measured by

Christ is Alive!

"It is hard to imagine anyone reading it without being caught up in the author's enthusiasm for his subject". *Church Times.* 75p

The Christian Response

An outline of a Christian attitude towards modern problems and a full christian life. 80p

Meet Christ and Live!

"Truly a tremendous book". *Church Army Review.* Paper 65p Rexine £1.50

Prayers of Life

"This is a most contemplative book, is profound without appearing to be so and is one of the best spiritual books to appear for a long time". *Doctrine and Life.* Paper 60p Rexine £1.50

ORDER FORM

To (Bookseller)

Please supply

.... MEET CHRIST AND LIVE! 65p

.... MEET CHRIST AND LIVE! (Rexine) £1.50

.... CHRIST IS ALIVE! 75p

.... THE CHRISTIAN RESPONSE 80p

.... PRAYERS OF LIFE 60p

.... PRAYERS OF LIFE (Rexine) £1.50

Name . . . .

Address . . . .

. . . .

Gill and Macmillan, 2 Belvedere Place, Dublin 1.

Michel ✿✿✿
Quoist

michel quoist

meet Christ and live!

michel quoist

PRAYERS OF LIFE

michel quoist

THE CHRISTIAN RESPONSE

michel quoist

CHRIST IS ALIVE!

the degree of personal detachment, by the degree of self-lessness. If you really want to make contact with others, empty yourself for the purpose of being filled. Create in yourself a *silence* for the purpose of hearing others. What will the other encounter when he comes into your life? If in you the other encounters the Lord, he will go away refreshed, experiencing a new peace and a new joy, for genuine contact should place us in the presence of God.

For a few moments each morning place yourself before the Lord, and in the obscurity of faith, welcome into your life for his sake all those whom you are to meet that day without as yet knowing what they will be like—love them in him. Then start out on your day at peace, expectant, ready to receive the invitations God addresses to you, ready to receive the other into your life. Someone rings your bell, someone is knocking at your door. Please pass me the hammer. Mrs Jones, are you at home? Mr Smith, may I have a word with you, please? A book, the newspaper, the radio, a film, a billboard, or a smile—a moment of silence, a cutting word, a lowered head. It is the Lord—these are invitations to make contact.

How to Talk to Others

We all experience the need to talk to someone else.
When overburdened with worries, or overcome by sorrow
or joy we feel a need to express ourselves. Words are the
means by which we are enabled to communicate with one

another. Those who find it difficult to express themselves often
suffer a great deal from their inability. Shyness, and a fear
of being misunderstood often paralyze this type of person
in conversation. The fact that there is no one willing to
listen to their problems only adds to their distress. In point
of fact there are very few who are willing to listen to their
brothers, for very few indeed can forget themselves
completely enough to hear.

Each one of us needs to say what is in his heart, to be pitied,
to be encouraged, to be helped. Listen to the other, listen
with genuine interest, without getting bored. Some have
never found themselves for lack of a real encounter with
someone who was willing to give his whole attention to
them, in short, simply to listen to them.

If you want to draw others to yourself, talk of what
interests them rather than of what interests you. Before
you can engage in authentic dialogue with the other, you
must first learn to listen. There are few who practise the art
of good listening because there are few who have become
selfless enough to escape from the perpetual noise of their
own self-intoxication: I quite understand, my friend, it's
the same with me. . . . While the other was speaking, we
were thinking of only ourselves. Don't interrupt the other
so that you can talk about yourself. Let him talk about
himself as long as he wants to.

If you're tempted to talk about yourself, isn't it because
you're thinking about yourself, because you're not giving
yourself unreservedly to the other? If you do talk about
yourself let it be only for the other so as to help him see his
own position more clearly, to reassure him that he's not
alone, but never speak of yourself in order to put the spot-
light on yourself, to make someone else feel insignificant.

If the other is silent, respect his silence, but tactfully give him the opportunity to speak. Ask him about his life, his interests, his plans, his problems. To speak profitably with the other it is often necessary to first ask him questions. Be careful not to let the other go away without having said all that he wanted to say. If he complains: Oh, he was too busy—that means that you didn't make yourself available enough to him. If he sighs: Oh, I didn't press the matter, his thoughts seemed to be elesewhere—that means that you were in fact *elsewhere*. Will he come back?

You find yourself worried, concerned with a number of problems, and then someone asks to speak to you. Calmly place all your worries and problems in the hands of the Lord.[1] Make this offering as often as you find it necessary and you will then be free to listen, to receive, to communicate. Also learn to take the initiative in your confrontation with the other. Offer a helping hand to get the conversation started. To offer a helping hand means to smile, to take someone else by the arm; it means to say: . . . and how is your baby? how did your plans turn out? and then . . . what happened after that? . . . Put yourself completely into each of these small efforts to lend a helping hand. Put all of the Lord's love into them for he is calling you to each of these encounters.

You put the medication on an abscess only after you've broken it and let it drain. If the other is experiencing difficulties, don't be in a rush to offer a solution. Tactfully help him to 'break the abscess.' Then a friendly word or a simple handshake will suffice—as a medication—for the worst is over. If you know how to listen, many will come to tell you what's in their heart. Give them your complete attention, remain silent and interested; perhaps before you have made a single suggestion, the other will have taken leave of you, at peace now that he has seen his way. For what he was unconsciously looking for was not advice but simply a presence.

If it is necessary for you to reply, don't be looking for an answer while the other is speaking, for he has need first of all of your attention and only afterwards of your advice. Look prayerfully to the Holy Spirit. It is the spirit of God who will give weight to your words, not mere eloquence. Authentic dialogue is possible only if you first establish a profound interior silence within yourself, a religious silence which will enable you to welcome the other into your life, because in the other and through him God approaches, and faith alone can dispose you for authentic dialogue with him.

The Encounter in Dialogue

A great deal of time is passed in discussion, a great many arguments are advanced and a good deal of energy is expended in the process. Discussion can be pursued almost anywhere—at home, at the office, at the factory, on the bus, in restaurants, at meetings, conferences, etc.
All too often we burn ourselves out in discussion, we get excited and angry, we hurt the other's feelings, we form factions. But all too rarely does truth win the day.
Why? If we are really at the service of the truth, how can we spread it abroad into the world in which we live?
What must we be so as to make a success of our discussions.

Have you ever noticed how frequently the persons engaged in a discussion withdraw more firmly convinced than ever that they are right? Why? Simply because arguments alone do not make up the whole of the discussion. Behind each argument stands a unique personality. Consequently a discussion is not simply an exchange of ideas or of positions, but most often it is a struggle between two personalities, and more specifically between two emotional involvements.

When you are engaged in discussion, think always of the other. If you succeed in 'destroying his arguments' and 'ridiculing his logic,' tell yourself that nine times out of ten you are at the same time hurting someone else's feelings. Have you won? No. You have only succeeded in helping the other to convince himself of what he was not previously sure. You are merely forcing him to find new arguments, stronger than the ones already advanced. But you keep up the struggle, your logic is inexorable, you back him up against the wall. At last he is reduced to silence. Did you not win this time? Not really. You have not yet overcome his emotional involvement. Deep down, he is saying to himself: Yes . . . but . . . , and from this 'but,' wounded feelings will sooner or later bring to light new reasons for a position which you thought effectively refuted.

You wound the other when you categorically condemn his position: Your arguments are *absolutely* untenable! What you say is *completely irrelevant*, that has *nothing* to do with the problem. You wound the other by your sarcasm: You haven't got your feet on the ground, my friend, you're out of step with the times; you're an incurable dreamer. You wound the other when you become vicious, even if you do so with a smile: You think like a child; you ought to have your head examined; you're absolutely mad. Stop insisting; you must first heal the wound you have caused. Apologize frankly and sincerely. If you haven't the courage, be quiet and look for a way of easing the hurt. If the other wounds you, it is because you have wounded him. Stop, relax, calm down, let your wounded feelings heal over.

If the other is forced to say: Obviously I don't have a university degree; I have not had the opportunity for much study; I haven't your experience; I'm too young to understand; you have humiliated him. Even if you are in fact superior, you should apologize. Acknowledge your incompetence in a certain field, acknowledge the merits of another point of view: Your opinion is very interesting indeed; my life is somewhat too intellectual, I don't have your experience with everyday realities; I'm already talking like an old man, your reaction is refreshing, it will help me . . . and then the other will no longer be merely a needy inferior but an equal who can give as well as receive. Do you really want to enter into discussion with the other? Start by trying to win his sympathy, and to win his sympathy first offer him your friendship. Should the other seem to you an adversary, a stranger, an enemy, don't waste your time with such considerations, turn your thoughts in prayer to the Lord and see him then as a friend, as a brother, as Christ himself.[1]

If the other puts himself wholeheartedly into the discussion, you do likewise. Perhaps you find it impossible to come to any agreement. Before speaking up, draw back from the problem, the arguments, the answer. Empty yourself. Your pride and self-love are evil counsellors. Your emotions will throw everything into confusion. You will have to re-enter the fray free of all prejudices, ready to listen to the arguments advanced on the other side.

Don't attach the same importance to every problem,

don't argue with equal vehemence over: which is the best washing detergent, which one washes whitest with the least wear on the clothes; or the best place to put the light switch in the hall; or the pros and cons of TV; or the problem of racial segregation. Before you speak, especially before exhausting yourself, draw back for a moment and judge the importance of the question with as much objectivity as possible and always begin on a positive note. Both of you will have to first be able to say yes instead of no, otherwise a mere mechanical opposition will be set up in which yes opposes no and no opposes yes.

The other exaggerates his position and so do you. That's why you find yourselves so far apart. In point of fact, you are quite close to one another, your opinions are not really opposed but very often simply complementary. Make an effort to understand the other's point of view on the question if you want him to be able to understand the one you are advancing. You can't give as much milk to a three-week-old baby as to one who is three months old, any more than you can feed the same thing to a sick man as you do to a healthy one. If you give steak to a baby, he won't be able to take it. You have to be able to determine how much of the truth the other is able to receive at this particular stage of his development. Be patient. By trying to give too much, you run the risk that the other will be unable to take any.

All of us change our viewpoints with the passage of time, sometimes overnight; rarely does it happen that someone changes his opinion because of the arguments of someone who has set out to win him over. Consequently, if owing to a genuine concern for the truth you have set out to make someone see it, don't say: I'm going to prove to him that he's wrong—but rather—I'm going to help him to discover the truth for himself. Most often, the other would be quite willing to accept *the* truth, but he refuses to accept *your* truth. Why try to monopolize the truth? It exists independently of you; nine times out of ten in making it your own you only serve to make it more difficult to see.

If you want to make a success of your discussions, forget yourself, respect the rights of the other, don't play the rich man who is merely giving alms to the poor. Rather be the friend who offers to work with the other in a common search for the truth. When it is a question of religious truth, never forget that Christianity is not fully demonstrable by means of logic, for before being a doctrine Christianity is a person. The truth is Jesus Christ.[2] Jesus Christ is not merely a topic of discussion, we must welcome him into our lives. 'To discuss religion' is above all to bear witness to the truth of Jesus Christ and thus to help the other to encounter him.

How to Help Others

There are many very well-intentioned people who wish to exert a good influence on others. However, they all too often start off on the wrong foot. When they ought to be giving their undivided attention to the other they find themselves preoccupied with what they are going to say or how they are going to act. Precisely what is their attitude both in regard to themselves and in regard to the other? If they feel themselves to be in every way superior to the

other, they are thereby doomed to failure. A pose of
condescending compassion will prove equally ineffectual.
Only humility can ultimately succeed, for only the humble
man is prepared to love the other and to seek out in him
those oftentimes hidden riches which are the gift of God.

If you would exert a good influence on the other, keep
before your eyes this golden rule: Always be positive
in your approach, never negative. The other is extremely
sensitive to the judgment of his friends and acquaintances.
A show of indifference or of a lack of confidence (or worse
still, of contempt) is sufficient to retard or even paralyze his
personal development.

If you would exert a good influence on the other, begin
with a show of unfeigned love; otherwise, you will get
nowhere. Place complete confidence in the other, come
what may. Show your admiration, there is always something about the other which should call forth your admiration in a visible, tangible way. Mere interior sentiments will
not suffice in this regard; they have to find visible expression. Silence always appears to the other as a sign of dis-
approval. The more anaemic his sense of purpose, the
more easily will he be led to discouragement by someone
else's silence. He thinks to himself: I don't count for much
in his estimation, he thinks I can't do it, he doesn't like me,
he despises me. It won't be long before he bitterly concludes: he's probably right, too.

Never say to yourself: I'm better than this fellow, rather
—he's better than I am in this particular regard. Thus
instead of discouraging him from the outset you will give
him the encouragement he needs, and hence you will be
helping him to grow to maturity. There is always a tendency for the other to be simply what you think and say

that he is. If you have nothing good to say about the other, it's no use for you to try to exert a good influence on him. Before making your first overture you will have to change your view of the other.

Praise, when sincerely given, has an almost magical power to transform. If you would see the other make progress towards full maturity, congratulate him on his accomplishments, but do it sincerely. There are always opportunities enough for such praise. Take a good look at the other, make a just evaluation of his good points, and his abilities, bring them into the open, for many are probably hidden, some due to neglect, others due to a defeatist attitude. To make them apparent to the other is to help him know himself as he really is. It is to help him towards salvation, for the Lord's condemnation falls on those who bury their talents.

In seeking out the good points in the other and in praising them at their proper worth, you are not being a hypocrite but rather you are praising the Father. When you seek to see the religious dimensions of the other, that is, when you approach him in the light of your faith, you are on the road that leads to God, for he is the giver of all good gifts.

Place complete confidence in the other, always and in all circumstances, despite appearances to the contrary, despite his disappointing failures. If you tell the other in so many words that he's a 'ne'er do well,' he'll become just that because you've convinced him that it's true, and so he gives up trying. If the other has stolen something, don't keep telling him he's a thief, but rather make it clear that basically he's not a thief at all, that he's made a mistake, but that he can do something to improve his present position.

If in spite of everything, you find it necessary to reprove him, to condemn a certain attitude or a certain action, begin by praising him for something worthwhile he's done. Reproof alone embitters the other, it hurts his feelings and even leads to discouragement. The other must be prepared to accept a reproof if it's to do any good. It's not a question of condoning evil but rather of encouraging good. Don't keep poking about in the ashes but rather look for the flickering coals and fan them into a blazing fire again. Be glad to see even the slightest sign of progress. Your approval will reveal to the other his own possibilities. Once he's attained a degree of self-confidence he'll be able to go much further faster.

If you would exert a good influence on the other, forget yourself. If you think that you can accomplish something for the other by yourself, you're only hindering your work. You can only do the spadework, open up possibilities. God has been busily at work and it is he who saves and redeems. To influence another means to go directly to the all-powerful Lord of love who alone transforms the heart. Do you find yourself discouraged by the all too apparent sins you see in the other? Recall to yourself the words of Saint Paul: 'Where the offence has abounded, grace has abounded yet more.'[1] No man ever falls so low that the love of God is powerless to raise him up. No one of us has the right to refuse his love and his confidence to one whom God loves and in whom God has placed his confidence.

What is Love?

*The life of man centres on love. In love's name and for
love's sake he works, he suffers, he struggles, he gives his
life, he even murders. The history of man could be read
as an unending quest for love, a history marked by brilliant
success and terrible failure. To love and to be loved in
return—herein lies the goal of each man's striving.
Man was made by love and for love. This is the inner
meaning of his existence, and it is only through love that
he finds personal fulfilment. Unfortunately, however, love
is a very misunderstood and much abused term. It is a term
which is used to describe relationships as different as day
and night. Man can set out on the road that leads to
genuine love only if he knows what he's looking for
and what love demands of him. In this life the road never
ends since the love for which man reaches always
exceeds his grasp.*

Hunger is a terrible scourge that kills millions of human
beings each year. Hunger for love is even more devastating,
destroying, as it does, untold human lives. All too often
man does not know how to love another. He thinks that he
loves the other when in fact he really loves only himself.

Along the road that leads to authentic love, many are
to be found who have stopped by the wayside mistakenly
thinking that they have reached the goal. If you are
'moved to tears' in the presence of suffering, if you find
your heart 'beating violently' in the presence of a certain
person, this is not love but simply emotion. If you are
overcome by her quiet strength or her lovely charms, if

you throw caution to the winds, this isn't love, it's simply shirking responsibility. If you find yourself ecstatically contemplating her beauty for the pleasure it gives you, if you find her intelligence absolutely extraordinary and her conversation brilliant, this isn't love, it's simply admiration. If you want nothing more than to look into her eyes, to hold her in your arms, to kiss her lips, if you would do anything to possess her body, this isn't love, it's simply desire or even lust. Love does not mean to be moved by another, to feel something towards another, to let oneself go, to admire another or desire another, to want to possess another. Love is essentially the gift of oneself to another and to others.

Love is not simply the equivalent of *feeling*.[1] If you wait until you're moved by feeling before loving another, you will love but few . . . and certainly not your enemies. Love is not the result of instinct but rather involves a conscious choice of the will directing us towards others and towards the gift of ourselves to them. Your love is too often clouded by self-love. Learn to lose yourself and to forget yourself: your love will become all the more pure. Hunger forces us to go out to buy bread. You find yourself going outside to see the evening sunset. You run after a friend whom you have just seen passing by your window. Desire, admiration, feeling can take you out of yourself and set you on the road to self-giving, but they are not in themselves love. The Lord offers them to you as means— this is particularly true in regard to the sexual attraction between husband and wife—to self-forgetfulness and ultimately love.

Love is a one-way street. It always moves away from self in the direction of the other. Every time that you use something or someone for your own ends, you cease to love, for you have ceased giving. You're moving in the wrong direction. Everything that you meet on your way through life is placed there to allow you to grow in love— your food for the growth of that life which is yours to give moment by moment; records, films, books which serve to enrich your personality and help you relax, thus enabling you to give still more; your studies which provide you with the knowledge you will need in the service of others; your work, your contribution to a better world, and your care and support for your family; a friend to make possible mutual self-giving and ultimately the gift of yourselves to others; your husband or wife so that together you may give new life; your child so that you can give him to the world and finally to another. . . .

Start out on the road of love today. Welcome into your life all that is good, but with a view to giving it to others. If you hold something or someone back, it is no longer possible for you to say that you love, for at the very moment that you took the other into your possession you ceased to love. You gather flowers in order to make a bouquet of them. You make the bouquet in order to give it to your beloved, for you do not want the flowers to wither and die in your hands but to bring joy to another. If you haven't the courage to give what you gather, don't bother, but simply continue on your way. In the same way, if you can not resist the temptation to hold back something or someone for yourself, then just pass by and continue on your way. You have to be able to renounce yourself if you want to love.[2] It is necessary to ask yourself frequently just how favourably your love compares with this notion of genuine love. Don't simply ask yourself: Is this love? Rather ask yourself: Does my love rest upon renunciation, self-forgetfulness, and self-giving?

We must always be careful to avoid equating the gift of things—money, a handshake, a kiss, even a bit of our time or our activity—with true love. Love demands not so much the giving of something as the giving of someone. Your love is authentically such when you give yourself or when your gift-giving is simply the expression of your self-giving.

What's the point of whistling for your dog if he's tied up? Why say: I'm giving myself, when in point of fact you are held captive by your attachment to something or to someone or even to yourself? If you're 'tied to' your possessions, or your plans, or your work, or your activity, or your comfort, or your associates, or your friends, for your own ends, you will never be able to give them, let alone give yourself. If you want to love you have to substitute detachment for attachment. Detachment, let me hasten to add, is not the equivalent of indifference. Quite the contrary, it implies esteem, admiration, appreciation and love. So much so that we find it impossible to hold back what we have and, even more so, what we are. We want to give all to the other. True love is the royal road to freedom in that it liberates us from things and, more important, from self.

He loves most fully who gives himself most completely. If you would know a love without reservation you must be prepared to give the whole of your life, that is, to die to self, for others and for the other. If you think that love is a relatively simple matter, you are greatly deceived. All love, if it is genuine, will sooner or later lead to the cross, for our sins make it difficult for us to forget ourselves and to die to self. Because of our sins, love demands that we be able to crucify ourselves for others. If you are out for what you can get, you will get nothing. You have to give. If you are motivated in your giving by the thought that it is only in this way that you will get anything, you will get nothing. If, however, you give without counting the cost, without expectation of a return, you will receive all.

The most difficult aspect of love is the element of risk involved, the demand for renunciation, the movement toward death . . . for the purpose of new life. It is this which makes us draw back from genuine love relation. You hesitate, deceived by the possibility of an immediate return on an investment in spurious forms of love. You're afraid of receiving nothing in return, you're satisfied with a half measure. True love, however, demands unqualified self-giving. In giving yourself to others you become rich in your poverty. It is love which brings us to fullness of life, for in detaching ourselves from self we discover the existence of others and are thereby enabled to become one with all the members of the human family.[3] Spurious forms of love, egoism and narcissism, for example, always lead to disappointment and frustration, for the failure to open out through gift-giving leads inevitably to the death of the person. The fruit of true love is joy, for through it the person opens out and is fulfilled in self-giving.

Jesus Christ is, needless to say, the perfect pattern of authentic love for in his life and death we see the most perfect self-giving, a self-giving which is perfectly free, because it was deliberately chosen. When you stop giving, you stop loving. When you stop loving, you stop growing, and unless you grow you will never attain personal fulfilment, you will never open out to receive the life of God. Love is the road that leads to God: it is through love that we encounter him.

What does it Mean to Love?

Contemporary psychology has made it abundantly clear that the root cause of most moral disorders is almost invariably a frustrated desire to love. Today's sociologists are asking themselves as they reflect upon contemporary society and the evils threatening it with dissolution: will men ever learn to love one another as brothers? It would seem then that the essential problem confronting us at the present time could be posed in the following way: will the love which leads to life be capable of overcoming the egoism which leads to death? Love alone is the key to the salvation of the human family.

Where love is active, sin is absent. Sin consists in a failure to love, in not loving sufficiently, in loving badly. It is possible for you to love all men, for love does not mean mere *feeling* but above all *willing*. It means to will the good of others, of all others without reservation.[1] But, you say, I can't stand so-and-so. Don't give up. Feelings of antipathy are instinctive. See your feelings for what they are. Don't try to pretend you feel differently than you really do. Accept your instinctive reaction as an unavoidable trial, then seek out in the other his good points. Try with all your strength to will his good. I really like her, you say. So much the better, it will be all the easier for you to love her. But don't rest content at the merely emotional level; use your natural inclinations to lead you to a relationship in which intelligence and will hold the upper hand. As long as you have not clearly chosen the other as a unique and irreplaceable value you run the risk of using the other for your own purposes rather than giving yourself in love to the other.

If your choice of a certain product is determined by the fact that you can get more trading stamps with it, it's hardly fair to say that you prefer the product on its own merits. If you spend a lot of time with a certain friend because you enjoy his company you can hardly call your attitude one motivated by love: you're looking for the extra trading stamps. If you have to admit that you no longer love the other, what you're in fact admitting is that you never really loved to begin with. It would be more correct to say that you no longer *feel* the same. If you continue to love someone who has disappointed you or hurt you, love has proven itself, for you love the other as he really is and not an image you have of him, nor for something you were hoping to get from him. You can only love the other if you accept him from the outset as he is, as he was, and without reserve as he will be.

If you find yourself saying: She's my whole life, and if this means that she absorbs all your time and energy, to the exclusion of everyone else, your love no longer rings true. If, however, you can honestly say that your love for the other has made you more responsive to others, then your love has the ring of authenticity. To love doesn't imply that you consider the other to have already arrived at the pinnacle of perfection. On the contrary, you should always feel that she has still further to go, you should be pained to see that she is not yet complete, you should want her to be striving for completion, you should give yourself without reserve to her for her completion.

When you have done all in your power to see that your

brothers are well fed and suitably housed, that they have opportunities for work, education, and recreation, when when you have struggled to help them attain personal freedom and assume responsibility for their lives, this will not yet be enough if you yourself have not learned to give your full attention to others, if you have not learned to welcome them into your life and to listen to them, if you have not learned to give yourself to them.

Love is the road that leads to life; egoism leads infallibly to death. Remember that you are called to a life of fruitfulness, not only to the physical fruitfulness which founds a family but a spiritual fruitfulness as well, a fruitfulness made possible by the gift of self to one's brothers. The branch which has fallen from the tree soon dries up and dies; in the same way, when unloved, the other finds himself condemned to solitude and to death. Should he find someone to hope in him, to believe in him, to love him, he will also find himself reunited to the human family through the medium of this one person. He will discover what it means to be called back to life. The man condemned to stagnation is the man whom no one will love. Never say of the other: nothing can be done with a fellow in the state he's in; you'll never get anything worthwhile out of him; it's hopeless, you're wasting your time, I've already tried everything. You may indeed have tried all the various tricks of the trade, but have you tried a generous, freely given love, a love which expects no return? Have you tried loving the other, because no matter who he is there is something good to be said for him, because God has loved him from all eternity?

To love your brother is, in some mysterious way, to call him to a new life, to awaken him from death, to reveal to him his real self. You'll never help your team to win if you hold the ball for yourself. You'll never reap a harvest if you don't first plant the seed in the ground. You'll never cause new life to be born unless you give your own.

What does it Mean to be Married?

How many young poeople there are who say to themselves on leaving the church: 'We're married at last, we've reached our goal, we have nothing before us now but joy.' What they do not realize is that this is just the beginning, that they have not reached their destination but are in reality just starting out for it. What they do not realize is that in order to become truly one they must strive each day to make their marriage what they want it to be. What they do not realize is that unless they give themselves to one another in God and through him they will all too soon become disillusioned with one another.

Once you've got your car going do you let go of the wheel and take your foot off the accelerator because you're moving now? No matter how long you've been married you are not yet and never will be perfectly married. Marriage is both a present reality and a goal to be attained. In marriage you must give yourselves to one another at all three levels of your human make-up: the physical, the emotional, and the spiritual. Don't play at being either an angel or an animal—be a man.[1] If they're to be of any use at all, a table has to stand on its legs, a bicycle on its wheels, and a roof on the house. You, in turn, must have respect for the hierarchical order of your human make-up, otherwise your home will be built on shifting sands.

Physical love, when left to its own devices, can not possibly be the visible manifestation of the spontaneous gift of oneself to the other, for unless the flesh is guided by the spirit it seeks only self-gratification. If you would love, the spirit must give direction to the body and the spirit of God must in turn give direction to the human spirit. A kiss means nothing if it is not an expression of love; by means of it you say to the other: I want to become one with you, I want to enrich you through the gift of myself. Sexual intercourse is the expression of the gift of self to the other, a gift made consciously, generously, and tenderly, a gift whose purpose is the gift of life to another. Consequently self-centred pleasure-seeking is out of the question here.

In order to give yourself you must first take possession of yourself, you must take possession of your body, your heart, your spirit. Self-conquest is a never-ending process, and this holds equally true of our self-giving and our love. As a result you will never be perfectly married to the other. It's difficult not to take anything for self, physically, emotionally, or spiritually; genuine love is not an easy attainment, but you have the whole of your life to help one another attain it.[2] Fallen human nature seeks to turn the world of things and of persons to its own profit, it seeks to turn you from the gift of self. Only the grace of Jesus Christ can restore to you the power to love authentically. Remember, however, that your life of love will always be marked by a sign of contradiction, the cross. This cross is a personal invitation from Christ to union. In dying to self, unite yourself to his death and he will unite you to his resurrection. You will never attain a life of genuine love unless a spirit of penance animates your life, and unless you frequently receive Christ into your life through the Eucharist.

You can find many couples making their way through life arm in arm, for physical union is relatively easy to attain. You will find far fewer who have achieved a union of hearts, for it is relatively difficult to love someone else with tenderness. Rarely will you encounter true spiritual union, for few are married in the spirit. Marriage in the spirit demands that you share all through a mutual confidence—all your ideas, your expressions, your needs, your doubts, your regrets, your plans, your dreams, your joys, your disappointments . . . all that comprises the inner world of the spirit. Marriage in the spirit leads you— through mutual give-and-take—to a common attitude of love toward your brothers and your God. Marriage in the spirit—through an ever-deepening knowledge of one another—brings you together before God, joined as two hands in prayer. Don't try to deceive the other nor yourself. See yourself as you really are, don't hesitate to reveal yourself to the other. It is only through mutual candour that you will become one. If you remain in the shadows of secrecy, you will never love. You must reveal to the other what lies behind external appearances.

The decision to love is a decision involving the dissolution of your individual autonomy, it is a decision involving emergence from solitude. You take the time to decide on the purchase of furniture, to discuss your budget, to make holiday plans. You keep track of your child's weight, you periodically record his height, you see how he's getting on in his studies. Do you ever take time out to see how far your married life has evolved? Are you more completely *one* today than you were yesterday? Will you be still more completely one tomorrow?

The flower must be transformed in order to become a fruit. The fruit must be transformed in order to become a seed. The seed must be transformed in order to become a living, thriving tree. If you would love, you must be transformed, for through the commitment involved in love you enter upon a new life. You will no longer see, feel, act, understand, or even pray in the same way. Yours is a shared life now, a life enriched through sharing with the other. Through your daily gift of love, you become mutually fruitful, not merely biologically but at every level of your make-up. You are born anew so that you may be slowly *re-created*. Consequently genuine love is indissoluble. A husband and wife through separation or divorce may sever their relationship with their children and with one another but they can never *unmarry* themselves.

Love moves from the body to the spirit, from the finite to the infinite, from the temporal to the eternal. Your love must gradually evolve and progress, from physical attraction and physical union you must grow to a union of hearts and then to a union of spirits which have become the dwelling place of God himself. If you marry only a body you will soon enough have exhausted its mysteries and you will find yourself looking for another. If you marry only a heart, you will soon enough have exhausted its depths and you will find yourself drawn by another. If you marry a *man* and even more so if you marry a *son of God*, then, if such is your desire, your love will be eternal. For it is the infinite, transcending as it does both husband and wife, which makes it possible for them to make their love eternal.

No one comes to knock at the door of an empty, dilapidated house. No one can drink from a dried-up well. Unless you have become for one another an inexhaustible well you will not be ready for love. Whether consciously or not, the intent of all love is union with God. As a result, perfect marriage is possible only within the context of the sacrament of marriage, the unfathomable mystery of Triune Love at work in two human persons who have been made one. If you live out the meaning of the sacrament of marriage, your relationship will hold inexhaustible possibilities for you, for you will give to one another the God who is love.

When is Three a Crowd?

Rare indeed is the man who does not waste at least some of his time in idly lamenting his situation. Most of us are dissatisfied with ourselves as we are and complain because we're not what we want to be.[1] In family life opportunities for dissatisfaction are only multiplied. Many husbands and wives feel that their marriages are failures, that they're just tolerating one another. If you want to make a success of your life together, you must strive to accept the other as he or she really is, as revealed by the passing of your days together; you must put an end to your mutual accusations; you must go beyond and overcome the apparent failure of your marriage.

Would you stop work on your house if the materials you received didn't correspond to your order? Would you throw away your knitting wool because it didn't come up to the manufacturer's claims? Would you abandon your children because they aren't all that you'd hoped they would be? Are you going to give up trying to build a life together because your husband isn't the knight in shining armour you'd been dreaming of or because your wife isn't the film star you had in mind? If you're still married to your dream, you're acting like an adolescent. Blame only yourself for your folly and stop blaming your husband or wife for not living up to your ideal. If you are disappointed with the match you've made and if you don't try to overcome these feelings, in spite of your best intentions, your dissatisfaction will out and you will drive the other still further away, for the other—in order to be brought closer to you—needs to experience your complete confidence. Your regrets are so many barriers keeping you apart when you should be growing closer together.

It's never too late to really 'marry' the one who shares bed and board with you. You only have to make up your mind to do it. Three is a crowd: your wife, yourself, and your dream. If you really want to get married, divorce your dream. If you can't build a castle you can at least build a hut, but you'll never be happy in your hut if you're still dreaming of living in a castle. Let's assume that you've made up your mind to break with your dream, to abandon your hopes for a castle. . . . Is this then the end of your illusions? No, this determination of itself will not be sufficient to dispel them once and for all. You will have to start by *forgiving* the other for you have never forgiven your husband or wife for not being equal to your dream. Offer your disappointment to God, offer to him your shattered dreams, your dissatisfaction, your rancour, your discouragement. Finally, accept the *real* person whom you have married, and your life together as it *really* is. It's not a question of remaking your world but of remaking your own attitudes.

Perhaps you have never genuinely loved your wife, desiring her only for your own selfish purposes. Perhaps she has never genuinely loved you, desiring you only for hers, and perhaps your two predominantly self-centred lives were for a moment brought together, giving you the illusion of love. Even if feeling disappeared long ago, you can still love her, you can still will her good. Her, you mean? Him, you mean? Don't pass judgment on the other but on yourself. If in fact she does not love you, love her even more generously. Rarely is anyone able for very long to resist the offer of genuine love. It is by loving that you help the other to love. You're always saying to yourself: She's been such a terrible disappointment. Say rather: I've been such a terrible disappointment to her. She's the one who started it? Well, then, you take your turn now: start over by loving her with a new generosity. If your glass is empty you can fill it up, but if it's full already. . . . It's our depth of spirit which measures our capacity to receive love.

You claim that she has every possible weak point. You used to say that she had every possible strong point. You're wrong on both scores. She has both weak and strong points, you should marry her as she is. It's not my fault, she's changed . . . and if she has changed, why are you so surprised? You married a woman of flesh and bone, not an immutable pose. Love implies a final not a fleeting choice. When you love a man, or a woman, you are always loving someone who is imperfect, someone who is sick, weak, sinful. . . . If you really love her you will heal her, you will strengthen her, you will save her. Love in some cases involves a whole lifetime of suffering. Those who decide to commit themselves to the other in love should reflect on this before they take the final step. The sacrament of marriage has consecrated your union, it also helps to perfect it each day. In your life together only Christ will be able to redeem you both from egoism and bring you to genuine love, but in order to come into your home, he has need of a 'yes,' today just as much as yesterday. Accepting your life together means accepting the other: it also means accepting Jesus Christ who alone can save you both.

The Mystery of Suffering

We see within us and about us in the world the
frightening and ubiquitous presence of suffering and of
death. Such has always been the situation of man.
Left to his own resources, man finds it impossible to fathom
the meaning of this mystery. Only the Christian faith
provides man with the key to understanding it, and thus
only the Christian faith can save him from despair.
Peace, however, lies at the end of a long and difficult road.
The man who knows suffering in his life ought not to be
surprised that he feels much closer to cursing God than to
praising him. However, he should at the same time believe
with all his strength that Jesus Christ will help him one
day, not only to understand the meaning of suffering,

but also to accept his own personal suffering. In this way
he will make suffering serve not only the interests of his
own salvation but that of the whole world.

Why is the rose inseparable from the thorns? Why does
the sea savagely devastate miles of coast? Why does the
radioactivity set free by man have to destroy the lives of
other men? Why does man's body corrupt? Why is the
heart of man as beset by suffering as his body? What lies
behind man's inhumanity to man? Why is suffering the
constant companion of man in his journey through life?

If your car's not working properly, you naturally
conclude that something is wrong with the engine. An
engine is built according to a specified design, and if you
put extraneous parts into it, you will either decrease its
efficiency or stop it altogether. Man, through sin, introduced disorder into the plan of the Father, and together
with it he introduced both suffering and death. Through
a loving obedience, the fruit of God's grace, man before
the sin lived a life of order and balance, experiencing no
conflict within himself, in his relations with others, or with
the world about him. Through egoism and pride man is
separated from God and condemned to conflict within
himself, with others, and with his world. The marriage
between spirit and matter, difficult even at best, is now
broken; the divorce between the two brings with it
struggle, suffering, and death. It is not owing to a decree of
the Father that man suffers and dies, it is owing to the freedom of man. 'For the wages of sin is death, but the gift of
God is life everlasting in Christ Jesus our Lord.'[1]

Could God not have prevented man from sinning?
Certainly, by taking away his freedom. Does a teacher
show his love for his students by giving them the answers

to their problems, for fear they'll make a mistake? Does a mother show her love for her baby by refusing to teach him to walk, for fear he'll fall? Does a father show his love for his son by forbidding him to go out, for fear he'll get into trouble? Would God have shown his love for man by taking away the possibility of a life of love freely choosen? When you love you don't take away the other's freedom so as to avoid his falling into evil, but rather you are willing to run the risk of error, of failure, of suffering. It is because God loves us that he has run the risk of our sinning.

You can often follow out the unfortunate consequences of your sin: your pride *wounds* the other, your egoism deprives him of something he wants or needs, your passions exploit and degrade the other. Alcoholism and debauchery cause innumerable physical and moral sufferings whose repercussions are impossible to delineate with any certainty. The culpable negligence of the upper classes and the wealthy nations, their egoism and racism are the cause of slums, hunger, sickness, misery, illiteracy. . . . You don't complain about being healthy even though you owe your health to others (your parents, those who grew your food, those who processed it, etc.). You don't complain about being educated even though much of your knowledge came from others (teachers, authors, etc.). Why do you complain then about sufferings which you didn't 'merit'?

If you accept the solidarity of the human family, you must accept it for better or for worse, for richer or for poorer. You are an integral part of the whole human family and of the whole cosmos, and you are continually coming under the influence of both. You are strictly dependent on the whole for your personal development, and yet at the same time you have a role to play in the life of the whole. Within the context of this total unity the most insignificant event affects the furthest limits of the whole of creation. When you sin, it is often impossible for you to determine precisely the consequences of your action in terms of the world's burden of pain. In the same way, when you suffer both mentally and physically, when disaster strikes the world in the form of floods, famines, wars, etc., it is impossible for you to pinpoint the origin of the disorder. Be willing to accept the mysterious solidarity of men and matter, but always keep in mind the fact that for every sin which appears in the world, somewhere a new suffering also makes its presence felt.

Could God possibly find pleasure in man's sin which is fundamentally a failure to love? How then could he possibly find pleasure in the suffering which is the inevitable consequence of sin? Since suffering reveals a profound disorder in the Father's plan of love, you should never merely resign yourself to suffering. Do everything in your power to fight against it—physical suffering; hygiene, proper diet, medicine, scientific progress of every kind . . . ; the suffering of the human family; justice and peace as international goals for all men . . .; the suffering of the human heart; education, love . . .; suffering resulting from the rebellious forces of nature; scientific research, technology, work. . . . When, out of love for others, you enlist in the struggle against suffering, you can be sure that you are entering into the plan of God. If you would be truly efficacious in this regard, lay the axe to the root—destroy sin. But this process of uprooting is never complete. Suffering remains a fact of our existence and will continue to do so. Will you find a way of using it to your own advantage or will it lead you into the murky night of despair?

Modern man makes increasingly extensive use of by-products; even harmful waste products are now utilized for the good of the human family. If faith throws light on the mystery of the origin of suffering, it also illumines the mystery of its *utilization* for the salvation of the world. Do you want to make suffering, the 'by-product' of sins, serve the interests of man's salvation? Ask Jesus Christ to show you how he made of suffering, by the power of his love, the raw material of redemption.

The Raw Material of Redemption

Suffering is neither the will nor the work of God but the work of man. Man, through his sin, has wedded himself to suffering: an intolerable marriage, had Jesus Christ not come to redeem suffering from its meaninglessness. Erected in the midst of the world by man's revolt, a huge cross overshadows not only the whole of humanity but the whole of the cosmos as well. However, the love of Jesus Christ for his Father and for all men has made of this cross the way that leads to resurrection.

Suffering has become man's inseparable travelling companion, and the moment of birth now marks the beginning of the movement towards death. What attitude are you going to adopt towards this situation? Rebel? Passively resign yourself to your fate? Deny the existence of suffering by trying to forget about it? Bemoan your sad fate and take it out on everyone else? Whatever the attitude you choose to adopt, you can not escape suffering any more than you can elude death.

Sometimes when confronted with someone else's suffering, you are tempted to think: I can't say that I'm sorry, he deserves it. God, precisely because he is our Father and loves us as his sons, never finds in our suffering a cause for rejoicing. He 'suffers' to see us suffer. After man had revolted from God through his sin and thus upset the order of creation, even after his refusal to love the God who is love, the Father did not abandon man to despair, but rather: 'He so loved the world that he sent his Son. . . . '

When Jesus entered the world he found there three 'creatures' not made by the hand of his heavenly Father —sin, suffering, and death. In order to restore man to a life of peace and love, and to restore the world to its original order, he had first to overcome sin, suffering, and death. Of your friend you say: I love him, I am deeply hurt when he sins, it grieves me to see him have to suffer. Such is the power of love to unite the lover to the beloved that he willingly identifies himself with the other. Because Jesus loved us with a love which transcended all limitations, he gathered us all together in himself, taking upon himself all our sins, undergoing all our sufferings, even dying our death. In the strongest sense of the word Jesus was the victim of his own love. As he hung on the cross he spoke to his heavenly Father: 'Into thy hands I commend my spirit,' that spirit loaded down with the harvest he had come to reap by means of his death. Father, I am taking upon myself the responsibility for the sins of all men and I am asking pardon for them. Father, I am offering to you the sufferings of all men in union with my own, I am offering their deaths in union with mine, accept them in expiation. In return the Father gave new life to his Son. The mystery of our redemption is as simple and yet as profound as that.

A mother accepts the pains of childbirth so that from her suffering new life may be born. Man can not bear an existence in which suffering has no meaning, in which he suffers to no purpose. If you are to suffer to some purpose, if your sufferings and those of all men are to have any meaning, they must be united to those of Jesus on the cross. Through Jesus Christ the Redeemer, useless, meaningless, intolerable suffering becomes the raw material of our redemption. It's not the suffering in itself which is redemptive, but the love of Jesus which gives inner meaning to the gift of suffering. You can not love suffering for its own sake; suffering is still an evil even after the coming of Christ. But you can love the opportunity it affords you of giving yourself and of saving both yourself and others. Your headache, your exhaustion, your physical pain, your confinement to a sickbed, your illness, your anguish, the difficulties of your work, your disappointments, your hurt feelings, your failures, your humiliations . . . Christ has already experienced all of your sufferings and has already offered them all to his Father—and the Father has already accepted them from the hands of his Son in reparation for your sins. In virtue of the love of Jesus Christ they have already redeemed the world. In each experience of suffering you can encounter your Saviour; through suffering he invites you to save the world in union with him. So bear your burden of suffering generously in union with him, and generously offer it in union with him.

All the sufferings of the human family represent in time and space the passion of Jesus Christ. The way of the Cross passes through all the battlefields of history, through all the slums, the hospitals, the working districts, the streets of your city or your village. . . . The way of the Cross passes through the lives of us all, but if you encounter Jesus on the way to Calvary and make up your mind to follow him, the way of the Cross will lead you ultimately to the Resurrection. The Saviour didn't invent or choose his cross. He rather accepted the one which the Jews and all of us placed on his shoulders. Before going out of your way to find the cross, learn to accept the sufferings each day brings. Choose the ordinary crosses of everyday life, not the impressive ones which will give you the false impression of being better than others. If you prune the tree merely for the sake of cutting the branches off, if you sow the seed merely to let it die, if you punish your child merely for the pleasure you get from seeing him suffer, you are without question psychologically unbalanced. Pruning, planting, and punishing all look to new growth and development as their ultimate aim. Consequently genuinely Christian asceticism is *never* without positive purpose but always involves renunciation for the purpose of a richer harvest.

Suffering is a continual reminder to man that he is a sinner. Suffering offered in Christ to the Father is a continual reminder to man that he has been redeemed, that suffering has taken on a meaning. Without suffering offered in union with Jesus Christ there is no possibility of forgiveness. Your daily suffering, when generously accepted and offered to the Father, becomes the most effective of your apostolic activities. Don't make a mockery of the meaning of the cross, don't make it a mere means for self-discipline, or a mere display of heroic endurance with a view to winning the applause of others. Don't, on the other hand, look upon it as the intolerable burden which saddens your daily journey through life.

The cross must be taken up daily by those who would save man and his world in union with Jesus Christ and his love.

Man: Collaborator with God

In light of the conditions under which many are forced to work, it's no great wonder that work is thought to be little more than an onerous burden. Some Christians are of the opinion that work is a punishment for sin whereas in point of fact work is both noble and ennobling. Through his work man collaborates with God in bringing creation to completion and in so doing he unites himself with the whole human family which is involved in the same task. We should not, however, be misled into thinking that sin has not insinuated itself into the world of work. Like the proverbial worm in the apple, sin has made its way into the world of work, and hence this world must also be redeemed. Only the Christian is able to bring Jesus Christ the Redeemer into this world and as a result into the cosmos as a whole. Through his work man collaborates with God not only in the work of creation but in that of redemption as well.

The Lord of creation has made men the lords of creation that together they might make it fruitful, that they might make use of it for their own needs, that they might offer it to him in adoration. The farmer sows the seed but God gives the increase. The Creator provides the stones but the mason builds the building. In all his work man is the collaborator of God. God then is present at the very heart of man's work. Work provides a meeting with God; it provides us with the opportunity to work together with him. That is why work can be a prayer. God, because he has made us to his image and likeness, has thereby shared with us his creativity.[1] Through your work you collaborate with him in the care and completion of creation.

The Father has such singular confidence in us that he has left the world's ultimate completion in our hands. He furnishes the necessary raw materials, he shares with us something of his power, but it is man himself who must plan and build, when he wills and in the way he wills. It is through your work that you attain self-completion, for through it you grow both physically and intellectually, through it you gradually increase your mastery over the world of nature, through it you become more and more creative, that is, you become more and more human. Through your work you link yourself to the community of the human family for you never create anything in complete isolation; you have need of others, of all men, in order to live and to build. The artist needs paint and brushes for his work and these are provided him by his brothers, and in order to provide the painter with his tools these brothers have need of others. . . . In order to cook one loaf of bread, in order to hammer in one nail, in order to write one letter, we depend upon the contributions of all our brothers.

You should work primarily not to feed your children, or to provide for your future, or to make money; you should work primarily to be of service to your brothers, and your brothers in turn will give you what you need to feed your children and to provide for your future. All too often work depersonalizes the individual; all too often it is a source of conflict between men. All too often it leaves the world of nature in ruins; all too often it is made to satisfy the greedy ambitions of a few; all too often it makes man not the collaborator but the rival of God. Work should help man to grow; it should knit the whole human family together in a common effort; it should transform the world to satisfy the needs of all men; it should give glory to God.

The Creator, after completing his work, 'saw that it was good.' Everything was in its proper place: the world was subject to man, the body was subject to the spirit, the spirit was subject to God in love. It is the rebellion of the spirit against God which results in the rebellion of the body against the spirit and the rebellion of the world against man. Nothing now is to be found in its proper place. Man must be 'repaired' in order for his world to be 'repaired.' God had commanded man to 'fill the earth and subdue it.' He now says: 'In sorrow shalt thou bring forth children.' [2] 'In the sweat of thy face shalt thou eat bread.' The bearing and rearing of a man, the particular work of woman, the 'bearing' and building of the world, the particular work of man, have now become difficult because of man's sin.

Work is not a punishment, the rearing of children is not a punishment, but these two areas of man's 'creativity' have become a source of much sorrow and suffering. Because we must 'repair' the work of the past this suffering can, if we are willing, become redemptive. Because of original sin and because of the sins which mark our daily existence, it is no longer possible to bring the work of creation to completion without at the same time redeeming it. Work can now be a source of immense joy, for the goal of redemptive work is resurrection. Your work needs to be redeemed, your work stands in need of Jesus Christ. Christ was himself a carpenter; in this way he first redeemed work through his own work. It's your vocation to bring the redemptive activity of Jesus Christ into the world of work: your intelligence, your heart, and your hands have all shared in the effects of Christian baptism and they must therefore make use of daily work to redeem the world, the world into which the Father has sent you precisely for this purpose. You must struggle in this world of work against all the injustice, all the depersonalization, all the conflict, all the hatred. . . . It's your vocation to sanctify the workers' struggle. Christ has gone before you into the midst of the fray, but if you want to encounter him and become one with him, you will have to commit yourself in a spirit of faith, hope, and love to your union, to its elections, to its committees, to its strikes. Your struggle will cease to be effective only when it ceases to be a struggle inspired by love.

You must be transformed, in Christ, into the image of the new man so that through your work and your commitment to the world of work, the world will be transformed into a 'new earth.' Sloth is nothing more than the refusal to take part with God in your own self-completion and that of your world. A bouquet arranged with all the finesse of the professional florist is, to be sure, a beautiful thing to see; but the child's poor bouquet, arranged not with professional skill perhaps but with a great deal of love, is infinitely more meaningful to a mother's heart. It makes little difference whether you find yourself in a position of importance and influence or in a humble and insignificant one as long as you are where you are meant to be, fulfilling the demands of *your* vocation in a spirit of love for the redemption of the world.

Don't be searching for an ultimate paradise on earth or you'll be sadly disappointed. You will achieve definitive self-fulfilment only in the next life, and the same holds true of the universe, which will achieve completion only with the resurrection of the body. This does not, however, dispense you from your obligation to struggle for the coming of this paradise, for the heavenly kingdom has its roots securely planted in the earthly one. You have to devote much of your time to the needs of the body but, in the last analysis, it's the spirit which is really the ultimate principle of authentic beauty. In the moment of the resurrection, your body will be transfigured in proportion to the interior transformation wrought by the Spirit. You are called by Christ to devote yourself generously to your work in the world and to strive continuously for excellence and even perfection in this work. However, the world of matter must be transformed by spirit. You are responsible for this transformation. In the resurrection, the beauty of creation will be due not only to scientific and technological achievement nor to the masterpieces of the world's geniuses, but also and especially, to the love with which the Lord's creation was brought to completion by man.

Your Commitment to Others

*Commitment is a word which has become increasingly
common of late. It is used to indicate the gift a man makes of
himself to his brothers, particularly in their struggle for a
more humane society in which to live and for improved
conditions under which to work. It is impossible for a man
to love God if he does not love his brothers, and he doesn't
truly love his brothers if he allows them to suffer without
lifting a finger to help. The further civilization advances,
the greater the hold which evil seems to have on political,
economic, and social life, and on our organizations, laws, and
way of life in general. This is, needless to say, an
unfathomable source of still greater suffering for man.
We can no longer be content with individual 'conversions'
in our efforts to liberate man. We must struggle today to
'convert' the institutions which constitute our society.
Nevertheless, the Christian must never forget that through
his commitment to the world he is attempting to bring
men to salvation and to build up the Kingdom of God.*

What would you think of someone who refused to help a
brother in danger of death? Jesus has told us that if we pass
by a suffering brother, we can not expect to possess eternal
life.[1] To know that every day men die of hunger, that men
live in hovels and slums or haven't a house of any kind,
that some, many in fact, are unemployed or receive next
to nothing for a salary, that some men are forced to work
under conditions little better than slavery, that many are

illiterate, ill, forgotten . . . , etc.—to know all this and to do nothing about it amounts to condemning ourselves to eternal death. In this life there are not several different ways of loving God, but only one: to give ourselves to our brothers. There are, however, many different ways of doing this.

If you seek to develop your *interior* life to the exclusion of your *exterior* life with your brothers, you are labouring under a serious misapprehension, for you can not hope to become one with Jesus Christ in the silence of your spirit if you leave the same Jesus Christ suffering and in need at your side. If the Father has placed you in the world and he clearly intends you to stay there, don't say to yourself: I have a special vocation to a higher way of life, or, I help others 'spiritually.' All about you, at home, at work, in your neighbourhood, your brothers are waiting for you and you can not evade the necessity of manifesting your love for them in a concrete fashion. It is quite true that God can ask of some that contemplation play a more important role in their lives than in the lives of others, but —save for certain clearly indicated exceptions—he never dispenses anyone from a love which does not find expression in the concrete. Religious who have lost their concern for other men as well as their concern for poverty of spirit (and material poverty) are religious who have lost the sense of God and of his love.

Beware of the subtle temptation to seek perfection by fleeing from the world of other men. You must, it is true, be striving for the heights,[2] but you also have to keep your feet solidly on the ground.[3] What you do in a concrete way to help your suffering brothers is evidence of the sincerity of your love for God. If you see a fight start, you should, of course, try to break it up, but you should also try to get those involved to come to some kind of understanding with one another. When an epidemic breaks out, we don't ordinarily just look after the sick, we also try to get at the causes of the outbreak. Our sufferings are the consequence of an almost infinite number of causes, and so we should not only help our suffering brothers, but we should also try to get at the root causes of these sufferings. Our efforts must envision the salvation of the whole of human life, the whole of contemporary society, not simply the individuals who live in this society, but the institutions which comprise it as well. You have to give expression to your love for your brothers by committing yourself to them. Your acts of service must be directed both to individuals and to the whole community of the human family, and this latter end can best be accomplished through the transformation of the institutions of society.

Perhaps a friend is not getting on too well, and you have been quite successful. If you make a generous sacrifice to help him, you are certainly performing a worthwhile and valuable act of service; but what about others in the same position, and what about the root causes of their difficulty? Acts of service which obviously help other individuals can prove deceptive, leading us to neglect the tremendous work which awaits us as mature Christians: in the larger context of the community, a work whose purpose must be the establishment of social institutions which respect the dignity of the human person and meet the demands of justice. Let's suppose that you have seen a robbery take place. If you don't do anything to stop it, or if you refuse to identify the thief, you become the criminal's accomplice and you deserve the same treatment as he. Through your life in society you are witness to many acts in which love and justice have no part at all, acts which bring suffering upon a great many others. If you don't speak up, if you do nothing, you become an accomplice: the guilt of these crimes rests upon your head as well.

Such is the world in which we live that we are sometimes forced to take part in what we know to be evil: some have to work in factories where bombs are made; some are forced to sell alcohol to those who they know will use it to excess; some have to take part in divorce proceedings; some, in order to secure needed contracts, must resort to bribes. . . . In all of these things the individual finds much cause for personal anguish and suffering. Participation in such situations can only be justified on the condition that the individual is striving in every possible way to transform this world of moral chaos. 'When confronted with human suffering under whatever form, strive, as far as your circumstances permit, not only to offer help but also to lay the axe to the root of the problem. However, do not be led into the opposite error of working solely at the causes of injustice without at the same time offering help to those who are now its victims. It is impossible to think of a man being genuinely good or just as long as he is not resolved to dedicate himself wholeheartedly, according to his abilities and opportunities, to the two aforementioned tasks.'[4]

If all had enough to eat, a roof over their heads, a car, a refrigerator . . . , if all had a decent education and a profession or trade . . . , if science and technology had gained mastery of nature, medicine had conquered cancer, polio, leprosy, in short, all diseases . . . , if the political and economic institutions of society were equally just to all, would the earth be a paradise of unalloyed happiness? No, not if the heart of man remained unchanged. You must strive in every way to make contemporary society a place where a truly human life can be lived, but you must at the same time guard against falling into the illusion that social reform, of itself, can guarantee man's salvation. What should you start with then—man and his attitudes, or society and its institutions? Seek to change them both simultaneously. But don't forget that, in the end, it is man who must be transformed for it is man's salvation which is at stake. Evil has made such inroads into the life of man that no man can even begin to root it out without the help of God. The world stands in needs of the Christian (that is, the man who has put on Christ), it stands in need of you if man *and* his society are to be redeemed from sin.

Man is a unified whole, and hence it is essential that with one and the same effort we try to save the whole man, not his body today and his soul tomorrow. You must save the world, this is your vocation as a man. You must save the world in Christ, this is your vocation as a Christian. These two vocations converge in the Christian man, for he is called at one and the same time to save the world and to save it in Christ. All of your commitments must be seen and lived in the light of your faith. You are both a member of the body of humanity and of the Mystical Body of Christ. Within the context of the whole organism, each member has a peculiar role to play. Don't let your whims and fancies guide your choice of apostolic work; rather let your choices be guided by a desire to do the Father's will. You have to take a long, hard look at the talents which the Lord has placed in your care, the circumstances into which he has sent you, those who have become your travelling companions through life. Then and only then, can you properly discern your particular vocation in the world. If you are called upon to work together with others, let yourself be helped and guided by your brothers, for it is only together with them that you will be able to save the world.

Many, because of a basic egocentricity, refuse to take part in the struggles of salvation history. Remember that it is better to run the risk of getting hurt in battle than to die of stagnation. The value of our commitment in the world is not to be measured by our position in the world, but by our willingness to be present to others, to be of service to them, in a word, by the love which we bring to our life in the world. Genuinely effective commitment in the world rests upon our commitment in faith, hope, and love, to the plan of God. Then and only then, can you say and mean: 'Our Father, who art in heaven, thy Kingdom come.'

You are your Brother's Keeper

The poverty and misery of the underdeveloped nations of the world is a frightening thing to see, but no less alarming is the indifference of the affluent nations of the world who refuse to give their all to save their suffering brothers. Each day the chasm separating the haves and the have-nots deepens. Only a failure to love can fully explain this. Today we stand on the brink of that chasm; tomorrow who knows? A Christian can not help but recognize his responsibility to co-operate with his brothers to do something about this situation. Let us never forget that the

Lord has commanded us to love one another as he has
loved us. Much of what will be said in this chapter has
been inspired by Abbé Pierre. Inasmuch as the bulk of this
material derives from personal conversations with
Abbé Pierre, references will of necessity be at a minimum.[1]

Today we are all well aware that two-thirds of the world's
population goes to bed hungry every night, that millions
are without suitable shelter, education, . . . If we do not
give our utmost to save these others from their misery, this
very poverty and misery will one day bear witness against
us before God. 'What hast thou done? The voice of thy
brother's blood crieth to me from the earth.'[2] When
confronted by open aggression, a nation automatically
mobilizes all its economic forces and personnel to save
itself. Confronted by evident poverty and misery, the
declared enemy of two-thirds of the world's population,
the one-third of the world which enjoys prosperity will
unquestionably perish unless it mobilizes all its forces.
'We can be absolutely certain that one war at least is a
just one, the war against poverty and misery.'[3]

By giving a little, we are able to save many. But
because we don't give all, we don't allow the underdeveloped nations to enjoy a decent standard of living and
a life worthy of a human being, that is, we don't allow them
to become the masters of their own destiny, for they must
still live off our alms. These men may one day rise up
against us to destroy us. Since we have not loved them
enough they will not love us at all. Because we give a little,
we allow many to attain a minimal standard of living.
But because we do not give all, we do not allow them to
find in themselves the means of overcoming their poverty
and misery. These men will become increasingly aware

that suffering is and will continue to be their lot in life and they will inevitably revolt.

Rarely do men hate those who have shown for them an unfeigned love, that is, those who have given themselves without reservation, without self-seeking, those who willingly give what they have without looking for or even expecting gratitude. Both the individual and society as well as the churches are clearly deaf to their responsibility when they seek to be of service first of all to the influential and the rich, instead of offering their services first and foremost to those who need them most: the suffering and the poor. The irresponsibility and immaturity of the affluent nations are indeed frightening. The same people who will spend millions to save *one* dying man lost on a snowy mountaintop, or to search for *one* victim of a shipwreck, will at the same time allow *millions* of others to die of starvation when a mere handful of rice would suffice to save them. What is the quickest way to bring together a husband and wife who have been drawn apart by constant bickering and argument? Their common devotion to a sick or dying child. Today men can be brought together in their neighbourhoods, in their cities, in their nations, throughout the world, only if they mobilize all their energies and resources to serve their suffering brothers.

As soon as a man makes an idol of a spiralling standard of living, he condemns himself to decadence and finally to death. Western man, the slave of increasingly tyrannical material wants, must be given a worthwhile aim in life or else he will simply disappear from the face of the earth. This will be effected either from within through personal disintegration, or from without by the onslaught of those many millions of suffering human beings who can not help but ultimately revolt. The challenge of the modern world can be met in only one way: it is no longer simply a question of struggling against class inequality; today our struggle must be directed against the terrifying injustice being done to whole nations.

'A man is saved only when he first becomes a saviour to others.'[4] Whoever you are, if you have come into contact with this book, even if you are poor, you are one of the privileged, because you live in a country enjoying certain advantages others do not enjoy. Every advantage, let us not forget, is also a responsibility. No matter what type of advantages you enjoy—money, material blessings, health, culture, education, faith—you are responsible for others. The greater your advantages, the greater your responsibility. You will be judged according to the use you have made of the advantages you possess. Suppose that one of your brothers was still alive but that you didn't know it. Suppose also that he was living in destitution and was in grave danger of death. Under such circumstances you would not of course be responsible for his situation. Suppose, however, that one day his existence, his whereabouts, and his present condition become known to you. If you did nothing to help him you would have failed to live up to your responsibility not only in the eyes of God but in the eyes of your fellow men as well.

Would you dare to say: I didn't beat my wife this week, I didn't put poison in her food . . . therefore I love her? Then don't say: I did nothing to hurt my neighbour this week . . . therefore, I love him, I've fulfilled the law. The Lord has commanded us not only not to do evil to our neighbour (the pagans could do as much) but to love our neighbour as ourselves. 'If loving my neighbour as myself does not mean that I should serve him before I think of myself, if he is less happy than I, what does it mean?'[5]

'We are to serve those who suffer more than we before we turn our thoughts to ourselves.'⁶ If you can be quite happy without these others, if your contemporaries can be quite happy without these others, then both you and your contemporaries are failing to live up to your responsibility, for 'thou shalt love thy neighbour as thyself' is not simply a 'counsel' of the gospel, but a commandment. The counsel reads: 'Go, sell what thou hast and follow me.' What you have above and beyond what you and yours need to live decently, no longer belongs to you but to these others. If you keep it from them, you are little more than a thief. If you give away, either directly or indirectly, your superfluities, you are not being charitable nor are you to be admired; you are simply fulfilling your obligation and nothing more.

To give of your abundance does not necessarily mean to distribute your goods to the poor, it also means to make what you have productive and fruitful for others. It's not a question of wanting to see all men reduced to equality, but of fighting against an excessive inequality, of 'converting' those who lay up treasure for themselves at the expense of their brothers. We were made to give of our abundance to one another out of love. If you see a drowning man in front of you, don't waste your breath saying: 'It's his fault, he should have learned how to swim.' Drag him out of the water first and then teach him how to swim. If he doesn't want to learn, you're still not quit of all responsibility; you have to persuade him and help him to want to learn.

Don't say to yourself or someone else (or of some other nation): It's his fault if he lives in poverty and misery, he ought to have got himself out of his trouble like I did. You're only condemning yourself as you speak. You have no right to steal what belongs to another just because he's not as gifted as you or because he hasn't had all your opportunities, or even because he's lazy or depraved. If you are more gifted, if you have had more opportunities, if you are more resourceful and virtuous . . . then you ought to help him in every possible way to become capable of saving himself. There is no end to loving others. You may not be 'personally' responsible for the world's poverty and misery, but you are collectively responsible. You may not be personally responsible for the subhuman living conditions of others, but you are jointly responsible, together with all those who enjoy the advantages of the 'rich' nations. And collective responsibility necessitates a collective effort to fulfil that responsibility.

Don't think to yourself: I can't do anything about it anyway, because you can do a great deal. Don't dream of doing great things, but be realistic about what you can do in your own circumstances. First and above all, commit yourself, within the context of your own life, to the struggle against injustice through professional organizations, political parties, unions. . . . Directly or indirectly you will be fighting against poverty and misery and for a better way of life. Regularly make a financial sacrifice to contribute to movements which are trying to better the lot of the less fortunate. Seek to become personally acquainted with the terrible misery in which the poor actually live, seek to make others acquainted with this situation. Public opinion is a potent weapon and it must be used to awaken the slumbering consciences of the more fortunate. *Every day* bring the suffering human family into your prayer. The commandment is for all, the counsel for some. More will be asked of some than of others, for the perfection of love is to make yourself *one of them,* to place yourself in the midst of the most unfortunate so that, together with them, at the heart of their poverty and misery, you may discover their way to salvation.

At the Last Judgment, in the presence of all the nations, what will the Lord say to you? 'I was hungry and you gave me to eat; I was thirsty and you gave me to drink; I was a stranger and you took me in; naked and you covered me; sick and you visited me; I was in prison and you came to me . . . ' or will he say: 'You did not give me to eat, you did not give me to drink, etc. . . . '[7] There in a nutshell is summed up the whole problem of the success or failure of your life (and that of the rich nations); if you ignore it, everything else is mere illusion and pretence.

PART FOUR

Man and His Life in Christ

The Double Point of View

*When modern man takes the time to reflect on his life in
the world, his characteristic reaction is either fright
or anguish. Even though he has deepened his scientific
knowledge of the world and has brought it under his control
in large measure through his technological skill, he finds
himself incapable of finding a meaning to his life in
the world. It is through faith that the Christian penetrates
to the heart of this mystery. However, all too many
'believers' reduce their faith to something merely human:
for the self-styled champion of orthodoxy faith becomes a
mere list of dogmas; for the professionally virtuous it
becomes a moral code; for the pious it becomes an
ensemble of rites and devotions.*
*How many look upon faith as the light which illumines
the whole of human life and gives it meaning, even in its
least pretentious aspects?*

Where you see only a drop of water, the scientist, by
means of his microscope, sees a world of life in continual
movement. Where you see only a 'thing,' the poet or the
artist sees a sign pointing to a higher, almost ineffable,
reality. Where many see only unrelated individuals
immersed in a confusion of unrelated events determined
solely by chance, the Christian sees sons of God growing
into the fullness of Christ and the Kingdom of God now
under construction. In the Incarnation heaven and earth
were indissolubly wed, and now each thing, each happen-
ing, each person must be seen from two points of view—

the earthly and the heavenly. Only the Christian is able to see man and his world in all their depth, for he alone sees them with the eyes of faith. Faith allows him to go to the heart of the world's mysterious reality, it allows him to transcend appearances.

Your senses and your reason enable you to see the world from the point of view of man; faith enables you to see the same world from the point of view of Christ. It is in the light of faith that you know God, the world, man, and yourself as he does. Faith is not a personal conquest; it is a gift, a gift from God. It is a gift from God in Jesus Christ which we receive at our baptism from the hands of the Church, his representative: 'What do you ask of the Church of God?—Faith.' However, if Jesus Christ has been given to you as your new life and light then you must prize his friendship and seek to grow in it each day. Faith implies encounter, encounter with Jesus Christ, so that you may see things as he does. 'I am the light of the world. He who follows me does not walk in the darkness, but will have the light of life.' [1]

Among those who call themselves believers there can be found those who think to themselves: I have *my* beliefs; I'm a good Christian, I teach my children the correct principles; faith is a great help, especially in times of crisis; I have *my* conscience; of course I'm a believer—I say my prayers, I go to Mass, I make my Easter duty, I don't eat meat on Friday. There are those also who think that they have lost their faith, or that their faith isn't as meaningful to them as it once was: my faith isn't as strong as it used to be; it just doesn't mean anything to me now; I don't feel anything, my faith is drying up; I have doubts about my faith; I've lost my faith. Both of these types rob faith of its real meaning, they are languishing in mediocrity and doubt or else they are living in illusion and error. They don't know what faith really is.

Faith is not a vague impression nor an uplifting feeling, nor is it a naïve optimism in the face of life's difficulties, nor is it meant to satisfy a need for security; nor is it an opinion, a moral code, the inevitable conclusion of a reasoning process, a scientific demonstration, a social habit inculcated through education. Faith is a grace (received in germ at baptism), that is, a gift of God. This grace makes it possible for us to encounter a person, Jesus Christ; it makes it possible for us to assent to the truth of what he has revealed; it gives us the certainty that his witness—both his teaching and his life—are true. Faith is a new perspective, the Christ-perspective on ourselves, others, the human family, matter, the movement of history, the cosmos, and God himself. Faith also demands commitment to the world revealed by this new perspective.

The Christian should think of the truth as a person before he thinks of it as a doctrine: 'I am the Truth.' In this life our commitment to this Person is measured by our commitment to his Church, which is Christ himself spread abroad and communicated. Reason can lead us in the direction of faith but it can never confer it. To be sure, we can demonstrate the credibility of what we believe, but reason of itself is unable to arrive at the fact of the Incarnation of God in Christ, or the unity of the divine nature in three Persons, or the filial adoption by God of this foreigner or that negro, or the completion of the work of creation through the building of this bridge, the birth of this child, or the completion of the mystery of the Redemption in this bedridden invalid. Imagination and emotion are even less able than reason to lead you to faith or to deepen faith once it has been given. Don't be alarmed if you never feel anything. On the contrary, you really enter upon the way of faith only when you renounce mere human reasoning and mere human feeling. If you would understand and see as God does you must be willing to die to the merely human.

Religious propaganda may indeed have its place but of itself it can never confer faith. The effectiveness of propaganda depends upon certain persuasive techniques, while faith, precisely because it is a gift of God, comes through prayer. Through propaganda we attempt to bring pressure to bear on someone else's freedom; faith, precisely because it is the personal response of man to God's call, requires fullness of freedom. In order to help your brother toward faith, don't waste your time with logical subtleties and arguments; rather love your brother and pray for him. It's not a question of persuading him but of communicating to him the Word of God through the personal witness of your own life. If you want to make a real success of your life, don't content yourself with a one-dimensional view of man. Encounter Christ in your life, commit yourself to him, learn to think as he does, to react as he would, to see as he sees, to live in imitation of him. He will reveal life's meaning to you and in him you will fulfil your divine destiny: life everlasting with the Father.

*Faith is a gift of God. 'No one can come to me unless
the Father who sent me draw him.'* [1] *However, because
faith is also a personal response on the part of man, he can,
with the help of God's grace, work to deepen his life of
faith. Everything we are and do has meaning and can be an
expression of our fidelity to Christ, a fidelity which is
lived in the community of the Church. To believe more fully
means to belong more completely to Christ, as communicated
to us in the gospel, our prayer life, the sacraments, and
the ordinary events of each day.*

In baptism we receive faith in the form of a seed, but a seed
is meant to develop into a plant and a plant is meant to
produce fruit. Your faith can grow, but not by continually
searching for new *reasons* for believing, nor by *imagining*
the goodness, the power, or the love of God, nor by trying
to *feel* the presence of God, nor by trying to convince
yourself that you should believe more unquestionably.
Your faith will grow if you commit yourself unreservedly
to the imitation of the divine Master, not only in respect
to clearly religious duties, but especially in your daily life,
in its every detail: 'If anyone would be my disciple, let
him follow me!' 'For in Christ Jesus neither circum-
cision is of any avail, nor uncircumcision, but faith which
works through charity.' [2]

Faith can also become anaemic and even die through
abandoning Jesus Christ for the worship of idols. What
are your particular idols: your body? your passions? your

intelligence? your attachment to some idea or to some method of doing your work or some particular devotion? your emotions? your feelings? your possessions? Which ones: your new suit? your transistor radio? your bike? your washing machine? your car? . . . or perhaps you're a compulsive worker because you'd rather 'burn out than rust out,' or perhaps money has become your god, or perhaps your efforts for better working conditions are little more than love of a good fight. No man can serve two masters. You'll have to make a choice. Faith is the choice for Jesus Christ . . . and all else that is good as well: but *for* Jesus Christ and the Kingdom of the Father. If your faith becomes anaemic, it always implies a turning in upon self, a refusal to commit yourself.

Are you having 'difficulties' in regard to your life of faith? Intellectual difficulties? Don't struggle with abstract ideas: first seek out Jesus Christ and then you will be able to reflect on your problems more calmly and more effectively with the help of his light. Difficulties over the Church? Don't be misled by appearances; bazaars, devotions, individual priests or sisters, a too-protective paternalism, condemnations . . . Seek out Jesus Christ. The Lord of the gospel and of the Eucharist will help you to understand that he is also the Lord of the Church. Moral difficulties? Seek out Jesus Christ. He will forgive you and offer a helping hand through the sacrament of penance. Your faith-perspective will take on new depth and clarity. If you want to see your way clearly you have to wipe off your glasses; if you want to see at any distance, you have to come out of your shell.

Be at peace, for if you try to be faithful and generous, your difficulties will prove to be only growing pains. Your difficulties can become stepping-stones to a deeper faith, for just as a dam forces the river to rise to a new level, our difficulties force us to rise to a new level of faith. However, the further you advance in the ways of faith, the further you will advance into the darkness of night, for in this life our God always remains a hidden God. Human reason is incapable of going beyond a rudimentary knowledge of this hidden God, in fact, it is an obstacle to true knowledge of God, the most subtle of obstacles, for as soon as we fall back into a one-dimensional view of others, of our lives, and of the world, our faith-perspective becomes anaemic.

Don't allow yourself to become a spiritual dwarf. Your life of faith must grow and develop just as your physical life does. Don't be satisfied with a child's faith when you're an adult. The adolescent discovers himself as a unique person, a world distinct from the world in which he lives. As the adolescent awakens to his own selfhood, he at first finds himself alone and afraid. Gradually, however, he attains a certain degree of self-assurance—in the measure that he grows in self-knowledge and self-discipline. For a period of his life he is too absorbed with his own problems to see beyond the frontiers of self, but when he reaches adulthood he discovers the world outside himself and also his place in that world. Generally speaking, the adolescent's faith centres upon the Christ of history, for the Christ of history is seen to be a person with whom the adolescent can establish a personal relationship. This approach naturally appeals to one whose attention is absorbed by a desire for friendship. The faith of the mature adult, preserving and developing this personal relationship of friendship, penetrates as well to the mystery of the whole Christ. It discovers Christ as the focal point of the historical movement; it discovers Christ's death and resurrection as giving meaning to this whole movement; it discovers Christ as the Head of the cosmos, at work in the world through his Spirit, building up the Kingdom of God.

If your faith is that of an adult, it will no longer influence only certain areas of your life. A division will no longer exist between your life as a Christian and your life in the world. Your whole life will become a peaceful but concerted effort to find your place in the plan of the Father as it unfolds in the world. This becomes possible only in Christ, with him and through him as we see him revealed to us in each word and each act of his life. You will have made a success of your life when you can sincerely say: 'For me to live is Christ.'

The Encounter with Jesus Christ

Man will never make a success of himself or his world unless he encounters Christ. Religion will be little more than empty formalism or a vague sentimentality or the quest for security or mere habit unless man learns to welcome Jesus Christ into his life. It is in the gospels that we meet him and it is there that we come to know him.
He awaits us there so that he may establish a mysterious dialogue with us through the medium of these pages.
Many Christians shamefully neglect the gospels, sometimes because they lack perseverance or generosity, but all too

*frequently because they don't know how to go about reading
Sacred Scripture. To rectify this situation it's not a question
of 'adapting' the gospel message, or of embroidering the
gospel narrative with fancy rhetoric; rather it's a
question of teaching contemporary man what the gospel is
and how it is to be read for his own spiritual growth.*

Do you find the gospels boring? Remember, you only
know certain passages from them, and these you have
heard largely at Sunday Mass, not always with perfect
attention. Perhaps you have opened the pages of your New
Testament only to find that you get nothing out of them.
The New Testament is not a book possessing magical
powers, a book that can be opened at random for the
purpose of finding there the solution to your pressing
problems. Perhaps you read the gospels frequently and
faithfully because the practice was highly recommended
to you by your parish priests, and yet you still get nothing
out of it. This is because you approach the New Testament
like any other book and you don't look for what you
should find there.

If you approach the gospels as a critical intellectual,[1] or
a historian, or an activist, if you are looking for an
emotional experience, or new ideas, religious platitudes,
or rules of morality, you are going about reading the
gospels in the wrong way, and you will be soon disappointed. You are like a Christian who would make a
very careful scrutiny of the ciborium, all the while ignoring
the presence of the host.

If you approach the gospels as if they contained merely
the words of men, you will find there only the thoughts
and wisdom of man. If, however, you approach the gospels
as the Word of God inspired by the Holy Spirit, you will

find there words of eternal life. Do you really want to enter into the spirit of the gospel message? Then you must approach in a spirit of reverence and generosity in order to hear and to see (that is, to contemplate) Jesus Christ who reveals himself here and now through the events of his life and the words he spoke.

Whether you realize it or not, you are hungry for the bread of the gospels. Complete silence frightens you, for when you leave the company of others, you hear only the sound of your own voice and this monologue disquiets and frightens you. The conversation of others is highly deceptive for their words are ephemeral and hence fail to fill your silence. You crave words of life, of eternal life. Respect this inner hunger you experience, this call of love asking to be loved by the God who is love. You are experiencing a hunger for the living Word, for the living Word who came down from heaven and is communicated by the gospels.

Perhaps you will object: I speak to God but he never answers. You are mistaken. From all eternity you have been called to dialogue with God. At every stage of human history God has sought to enter into dialogue with man: 'God, who at sundry times and in diverse manners spoke in times past to the fathers by the prophets, last of all in these days has spoken to us by his Son. . . .'[2] If you find yourself complaining of the silence of God, it's because you don't open your ears and your heart to the words of the gospels. It is in the gospels that God wishes to enter into conversation with you. Answer his call. It is in this way that you will be able to enter into conversation with Jesus Christ. The lover finds his joy in revealing himself more and more fully to his beloved. God, who so loved the world that he gave his only-begotten Son, delights in revealing himself to man through the medium of Sacred Scripture. Are you attentive to this revelation God makes of himself in Jesus Christ? Would you let your fiancée's letter lie unopened on your desk? Why then do you let the gospels stand unopened on your bookshelves? Today a letter has arrived for you from the Son of God. What is Jesus Christ saying to you for today?

Jesus Christ left his Body to the Church, but he also left his words, for Jesus lives in the Eucharist and speaks in the gospels. Hence, approach the gospels in the same spirit that you approach the Eucharist. You can receive these words of life over and over again; their depths are unfathomable, for 'the word of God is living and efficient and keener than any two-edged sword. . . .' [3]

What's the point of taking the receiver off the hook if your telephone isn't connected yet? What's the point of opening the pages of the gospels if you haven't first prayed so that you'll be 'connected up' with the divine through faith? You can't encounter the Lord and hope to understand his word unless you've first asked the Father to be your guide and the Spirit to be your interpreter. Jesus Christ doesn't speak the same language as you and that's why you find it hard to understand him. You talk about being effective and he says then you'll have to bear the cross. You talk about exerting influence in the world and he says then you'll have to be the least of all. You talk about being powerful and he says then you'll have to become a child. You talk about being rich and he says then you'll have to be poor. Jesus Christ doesn't have the same ideas you have, nor the same mentality, nor the same attitude to life, nor does he use the same methods, nor esteem the same values. It's difficult to understand one another when you don't speak the same language. You're going to have to change and you're first going to have to accept that fact.

If you find yourself saying, after reading the gospels: I wish so-and-so would read that passage . . . , you haven't understood the real import of the passage, for it's you to whom the Lord is speaking. If you don't find yourself saying: Be merciful to me, Lord, a sinner; Lord, here I am at your service; the Word of God has not hit its mark, for it was aimed at you. Precisely because you read your favourite newspaper with regularity you begin to adopt its ideas and attitudes as your own. Precisely because you admire a man, you soon begin to react and to think as he does. Precisely because you like a friend, you begin to act like him and imitate him. If you make the gospels a regular reading companion, slowly you will begin to think, to feel, to judge as Christ does. In becoming familiar with the gospel you must of necessity begin to resemble Jesus Christ.

'To proclaim the gospel message by everything you are and do'[4] does not mean to sermonize at your factory, or your office, or your school. Rather, it means to be so filled with the spirit of the gospels that your desires, your thoughts, your values, your attitudes have become those of Christ. The more you meditate on the gospel message, the more Christlike, the more apostolic you will become. You don't say: I've just eaten and yet I don't feel any stronger. Then don't say to yourself: I've been reading the gospels each day for the last week and nothing is changed in my life. What response do you expect from your show of love other than to be loved in return? The gifts will come in due time. Don't always be trying to get something out of everything you do. Meditate on the gospels in a spirit of generosity; simply try to be faithful to God's revelation of his love for you. If you try to "apply" the gospel message to your life in some artificial way, it will not be the gospel which inspires your life but some merely human conception of it. Let the Holy Spirit breathe where he will, and in his own good time. Let him lead the way for you. If you are attentive and faithful to his guidance, you will be surprised to find him making his presence felt in your life with unexpected frequency. This is what it means for the gospel to find expression in your life.

If you happen to belong to a Bible study group, tell yourself that it's not a question of commenting on the gospel, or of exchanging ideas on a certain passage, but rather of communicating to one another what the Holy Spirit has revealed to you.[5] Meditation on the gospel is not something that you do by yourself. You, on your side, must recollect yourself and dispose yourself to receive Christ. The Holy Spirit, on his side, must lead you to the Lord and transform you in him. If you find yourself saying: I'll never make any progress, I don't get anything out of reading the gospels—it's either because you're thinking solely of your own activity, or because you judge the activity of the Holy Spirit according to merely human standards. Never get discouraged. If you have done your utmost, the Holy Spirit will bring your efforts to a fruitful conclusion. Coming to the gospel means above all disposing yourself to welcome the action of God into your life, for you are not a Christian because you love God but because you believe that God loves you and because you let yourself be loved by him. Come then to the gospels; don't break your appointment with God.

The man who sincerely wants to live the Christian life is not content to restrict this life to certain well-defined

limits, to certain clearly religious acts, to the mere minimum which satisfies the letter of the law. The authentic
Christian wants his faith to develop to maturity; he wants
his faith to give meaning to every aspect of human
existence, his own as well as that of the whole human
family.

The real intent of religion is to bind man and his world
to God. This the Christian attempts to accomplish at each
moment of his life. He seeks to encounter Christ in each
moment and in each circumstance, at the very heart of
the concrete situation into which he has been *sent*. The
present moment is not to be thought of as an ambush
prepared by a God of wrath, but rather as a rendezvous
prepared by a God of love.

To live the Christian life to the full the Christian must
bring a new point of view to bear on his own life, on that of
his brothers, and on that of his world. His view must be
one of faith and of hope, evoking a response of love. He
must seek to discover 'the grand design' and the real
dimensions of each 'event' in his life; he must 'review'
his whole life in the light of his faith.

The World as the Father
Sees It

*Here is a meditation which seeks to inculcate a faith-perspective
for the whole of your daily experience. Unless you make a
daily effort to see the world as God sees it, you will never get*

beyond mere appearances, you will never see the
movement of human history as a movement of salvation.

Lord, I want to go beyond the narrow confines of the world of time; I want to be purified and to see with your eyes. Then I would see man and his world and his history as the Father sees them. Then I would see in the staggering technological changes and the incessant movement of contemporary society the growth of your Body, coming to maturity through the work of your Spirit. Then I would see the Father's love working out its purposes in history, reconciling heaven and earth in your Person. Then I would see that each day, each event, each part fits into the structure of the whole; that each man, each group, each thing has its proper place. Then I would see the whole of human life and history spread out before me, with all its joys and sorrows. Then I would see the interpenetration of matter and spirit, the struggle between love and hate, between grace and sin.

Then I would understand that I have a part to play in salvation history, the history of God's love at work in the world, a history which began at creation and which will be consummated only with the resurrection of the body. It is then that you will come before the Father, proclaiming for all to hear: It is consummated, I am Alpha, I am Omega, the beginning and the end of all things. Then I would understand that all is of a piece, that in you and through you and with you, the whole of human history is caught up in the movement leading to participation in the divine life. Then I would understand that nothing is profane—no thing, no person, no event—but that, on the contrary, all have been consecrated by God from the very beginning and that all must yet be consecrated by man sharing the life of God. Then I would understand that my life, as insignificant as it may seem within the context of this magnificent Body, is in reality indispensable to the Father's plan. Then, falling down on my knees in wonder, Lord, I would praise you as I beheld the mystery of salvation history, a history which, in spite of sin, is one long movement of love, divine love in search of man and man in search of divine fulfilment.

Lord, I want to go beyond the narrow confines of the world of time; I want to be purified and to see with your eyes.

Behold,
I make all things New

Each event is but a part of the total movement of history
but like this movement each event in it is pregnant with meaning.
Only the Christian can plumb the depths of this
meaning as he alone sees with the eyes of faith.
However, this faith has to be continually brought into play and
we must be continually prepared to respond to its demands.

I wasn't paying attention! It'll pass! It has to be that way! It was inevitable! I can't do a thing about it! That's the way things are! It happened purely by chance!

You have no right to talk like that. You are making a serious mistake when you do. Nothing is profane, no matter what happens. A new world is emerging from the chaos of sin: the Kingdom of the Father is in the process of construction. The human family had been scattered far and wide; it is now being gathered together into one Body: it is the mystical Christ in the process of formation. Each event is a moment of that gigantic process.

The smallest stone, the smallest of plants, are to be reverenced, for God is there, through his activity. Even the lowest level of life is to be reverenced for it in some way shares in the mystery of Christ. The importance of each event is not to be gauged by its external brilliance but by its hidden depths. Your daily dread, the bread which nourishes you each moment of your life, is the event, the events which form the texture of human existence. In the Eucharist Jesus invites you to receive his Body. In the gospel he invites you to receive his Word. In the events of your life he invites you to share in his work in the world. Listen attentively to the demands of the present moment, for in them you will find the Lord's will manifested. The exigencies of the present moment make concrete the demands of the gospel message. If each event in our lives is rooted in infinity, it is also as wide as the frontiers of the human family, for the most insignificant of events reaches out to embrace your brothers, scattered though they be throughout time and space. The response you make to the circumstances of the present moment spells happiness or misery not only for yourself but for all your brothers.

Each event in your life is a call, a sign, an invitation from both man and God. In giving the whole of your attention to these circumstances you are giving your attention to your brothers and to God. By being present to these circumstances you are making yourself available to your brothers and to God. By responding to these circumstances, you are giving yourself in love to your brothers and to

God. If you are not fully one with your brothers in Christ, if you find that your efforts are ineffectual, it's because you have not yet encountered the Lord in your circumstances; in the last analysis, it may be because you do not yet see that each event veils a profound mystery. In order to give a Christian's response to these circumstances you must learn to see them in the light of faith.

Reviewing
your Personal Life

If you take the trouble to look back over your day in the light of your faith two or three times a week, or better yet each night,[1] alone, or, if you're married, together with your wife, you can rest assured that you will eventually attain to a mature Christian life.

Even at the human level, you do not live your life to the full.[2] At the supernatural level, your distracted and self-seeking prayer life: Lord, I offer you what *I've done*; Lord, help me (to accomplish what *I've decided to do*)—does not constitute a genuine *life* of faith. If you really want to live your everyday life in the light of your faith, if you really want to evaluate it in the light of your hope for eternal life, if you really want to live it in loving union with Jesus Christ and your brothers, you must learn to review it from a new standpoint. From this new standpoint, worldly success will soon count for little.

The athlete has to train for many long and hard hours, the craftsman has to spend long hours learning his trade, the artist fails many times before producing a master-piece. Why then are you unwilling to make any effort to live an authentically Christian life? The review in question here is not an examination of conscience[3] nor is it a means of checking on your good resolutions, nor a training pro-gramme leading to greater attentiveness, nor a means of personalizing your activity; rather it is a new point of view (a review) on your life; it is a point of view illumined by faith, and hence it transcends both sense and reason.[4]

If you close your heart, you can approach the Eucharist without entering into a profounder friendship with Jesus Christ, you can read the gospels without hearing the Word of Jesus Christ, you can review your life without seeing Jesus Christ there inviting you to share his work. Before you begin your review, ask God to purify your heart so that you can see things as he does. The astronomer doesn't try to observe the whole universe at once; he marks out a corner of the heavens for special study. The biologist, for his part, isolates various bacteria for micro-scopic study. If you want to accomplish anything, concentrate your attention on a single area of your life at a time.

Today you met Jim. What was Christ asking of you in that encounter? Today you got on the bus for work. What was Christ expecting from you and from the others there with you for those few moments? Today you read a certain news item in the daily paper. What was Christ trying to tell you through your paper? Today at work a strike proposal was discussed. How did your fellow workers react? What was Jesus Christ telling you through this situation? Your neighbour told you . . . on your football team Sunday . . . , on the radio you just heard that . . . , the union is going to . . . , the butcher's little girl . . . , at the house across the street yesterday . . . , in two weeks the elections . . . , etc. Each situation of your daily life provides the raw material for your review; each situation provides an opportunity for collaborating with Jesus Christ in his salvific work; each situation can become an encounter with the Lord. Ask him to make each situation such an encounter and ask him also to help you to fulfil his purpose in these circumstances.

All love begins with knowledge. In your confrontation with the present moment, begin to recognize Jesus Christ present in your life and in the movement of history. The present moment is a sign. You will have to discover what the Lord is seeking to indicate to you through this sign. In order to understand a foreigner you first have to learn his language, his mentality, his customs. In order to interpret your life and the life of your world as signs from God, you must become familiar with the attitudes, the words, the life of Jesus Christ. If you want your review to accomplish anything in your life, make the gospels regular required reading.[5] You will not always be able to understand what God is asking of you, for his voice will sometimes fail to crack the communication barrier erected by human insensitivity and sin. Ask his forgiveness and in the darkness of faith, silently praise him.

God speaks to you in the gospels and he awaits a response from you. He also speaks to you through the circumstances of your life, inviting you to dialogue with him. Your review of your life should lead spontaneously to prayer: a four-dimensional prayer of praise, thanksgiving, penance, and petition. If God speaks to you through the circumstances of your life, it's in order to invite you to work with him and in him. Through your review of your life, your work in the world is no longer merely a matter of technical skill, nor a quest for 'ways' of fulfilling your apostolic obligations, but rather a response to the will of God, a response which takes its point of departure from the concrete realities of everyday life. You must learn obedience to the Lord in the school of real life.

If you are sincere and faithful in reviewing your life, you will encounter not only the Christ of history but also the whole Christ, Head and members, the Mystical Body growing to perfection throughout the whole course of human history. You will soon come to see your life as part of the total salvific plan of the Father. You will live with the life of Christ by uniting yourself, through the circumstances of your life, to his mysteries made present in history. You will learn to make yourself available to others by seeking everywhere the will of God. You will, through your work and in the company of your brothers, help to bring to completion the creative and redemptive work of God. Each day you will move one step closer to attaining the fullness of Christ.

Reviewing your Group Life

No man is an island, each lives as a member of the whole human family. This holds true even more so for the Christian, for he lives always and everywhere in the

*context of the Church. If you strive to live this communal
life you will be living according to the plan of the Father
who wills to see all his sons united into one family.
Review of our own personal lives should always lead to a
review of your life in the totality of the group. This
is especially true in the field of Catholic Action when a
particular group is at work within a particular community.*

Your review as a member of a group bears certain
resemblances to your review of your own personal life;
however, it is made in the context of a mutual commitment
to some work in the world. Review as a group effort is not
a get-together for the purpose of rehashing the happenings
of the past week, nor is it a court set up in judgment over
others, nor is it a business meeting for the purpose of
reporting on past accomplishments, nor is it a collective
check on private resolutions. It involves instead communal
consideration, illumined by the light of faith, of a situation
which affects the community in which the group works, a
situation in which one of the members of the group finds
himself involved.

Because every situation veils an invitation from God,
it demands an active response—a personal response, a
group response, a community response.[1] If you really
want to encounter the Lord you must first prepare yourself
for such an encounter. Every attempt at review presupposes a degree of recollection; it must take its point of
departure in a humble prayer of petition and find its
fulfilment in a prayer of thanksgiving.

When confronted with a new situation, first review your
own attitude and only then that of the community in
which you are working. In regard to your commitment to
this work, don't waste your time attempting to explain

what your commitment means, don't waste your time trying to justify the position you've taken, rather review *your attitude* as a Christian *within the context of this commitment*. If you find yourself saying: I won't get anything out of that—it's simply because you're not willing to put anything into it. Don't look for what you can get out of the situation, but rather try to see what you can contribute to it.

Group review requires that you learn to speak when the occasion arises and to keep silent as well; hence you must avoid speaking out either too much or too little. Remember too that group review will succeed only if each of the members of the group has made review a daily practice in his own personal life.

The Church entrusts to lay apostolate groups the work of preaching the gospel of Jesus Christ in their own circumstances. If you take part in an organized group, *you and your brothers* are helping to bring the Church into your own milieu and at the same time you are helping to bring your milieu into the life of the Church. Never forget that the Holy Spirit will be with your group helping you to come to a knowledge of God's will for you in your own circumstances.

Group review provides a means by which the circumstances of your life in the world can be brought into contact with the life of the Church. This group review on the part of earnest laymen can be of great service to priests, enabling them to mediate the Word of God more effectively to the contemporary world. In your group review, try first to see what has already been accomplished in the circumstances in which you wish to exercise the apostolate —the goodness of those with whom you live and work, their innate sense of brotherhood, their desire for social

justice . . . , all, in a word, which is already the work of
God in the world, although it does not appear as such to
those involved. If you habitually make such considerations
your point of departure for action, you will be less tempted
to see only *your activity* and you will seek rather to collaborate with the activity of God.

You mustn't content yourself with SEEING your situation in the light of your faith, of EVALUATING it as a
sign from God, of ACTING in response to his will. You
must also help your brothers to review their own lives
for themselves, for they have also been invited by the
Lord to encounter him in the circumstances of their lives.
The deeper your group's insights into the things of God,
the greater the influence your group will be able to bring
to bear on the situation in which it finds itself, for you will
be better able to bear witness to the Word of God to those
with whom you live and work. The Lord is close to them
in all the circumstances of their lives, but they need the
light of faith and the power of love before they will be
able to recognize him and follow him on their own
initiative.

Prayer is an Act of Faith

Among those who do not pray or pray little or badly
there are to be found some who do not believe in prayer,
thinking that activity alone is more urgent and more useful.
There are some others who look upon prayer as a magical
incantation and hence they use it to satisfy all their needs

and wants, even the most overtly material ones. There are
some others who would like to pray but who claim that they
can't or that they don't know how. In all these cases,
it would seem that prayer is not being properly evaluated for
what it is—an act of faith. Modern man, the slave of
efficiency and utility—sometimes in spite of himself—
tends to think of prayer in terms of profit and loss.
Prayer can not be understood in such pragmatic terms and
such a view can never lead to an authentic prayer life.
The modern world has, nonetheless, an urgent need for a
life of prayer. Unless the members of a technological society
are also men of adoration and praise, technology will
enslave and ultimately destroy them.

You would never think of saying: I don't have to bother
to show my love to my wife any more, she knows I love
her. Then don't say: I don't have to talk to God, he knows
that I love him. You would never think of saying: I
haven't time to spend with my wife, but what's the difference, I'm working for her. Then don't say: I haven't time
to pray, but that doesn't make any difference, I offer my
work up and that's a prayer. Love demands that you stop
for a while. If you love, you must find the time to love.
To pray means to stop for a while; it means to give some
of your time to God, each day, each week. In the modern
world, Sunday has become the day that is set aside, the
day we reserve for ourselves. Let us not forget that in
reality it is the Lord's day.

If your fiancée gets fewer and fewer letters from you,
she knows that your affection is beginning to flag. If you
don't "correspond" with God any longer, this may be the
danger signal. If you no longer take the trouble to pray,
you will soon find that you no longer recognize and hear

Jesus Christ talking to you through the circumstances of your life, for in order to see him and understand what he says, you have to look for him and listen to him in those brief daily encounters which prayer makes possible. Prayer is a turning to God and without it our lives become progressively more self-centred. Through prayer we bind ourselves to God and without it we close ourselves up in our own solitude. Man needs a god and without prayer he becomes his own god. If your life is lived far from God, eventually you will come to the conclusion that you can live without him. If you learn to live without him, eventually you will forget him. If you forget him, you will finally conclude that he doesn't even exist.

If you're always looking for something from the beloved, you're not a lover but a businessman. Your prayer is all too often little more than a business deal with God . . . you want it to yield a return. Your prayer life is only one-dimensional because it consists solely in the prayer of petition. The fundamental attitude of authentic prayer is personal presence and generosity: Our Father, who art in heaven, hallowed be thy name. Prayer is not merely gift-getting; it is also gift-giving. In prayer you should give to God the life of the world, your own life, and yourself. Even when your prayer is not directly aimed at gift-getting, you still may be looking for an emotional experience from prayer. Very often you don't have any such experience and so you give up: I don't get anything out of it, I feel like I'm talking into the void, I don't feel anything. Without a special grace you won't feel anything in prayer. Emotion is situated on the sense level, but prayer puts us in the presence of One who is beyond sense experience. You will never attain to a life of authentic prayer so long as you are looking for an emotional experience.

Very often our prayer will consist simply in accepting bordeom and distraction as we stand before God. When you are overtired, burdened by responsibilities and cares, overwhelmed with work, continually busy, persistently interrupted by others, forget yourself and stop for a moment; place everything in God's hands, acknowledge man's inadequacy before the infinite God, gladly "waste your time" before him. This will require an act of faith, of adoration, and of love, and so you have already laid the foundation for prayer. You have to want to pray, and to want to pray is to pray. Try to put yourself in the presence of God, try again. Set a definite period of time aside for prayer and don't say: I can't pray, I don't know how to pray, for as long as you are trying to pray, you are praying. On your part, the value of your prayer depends upon the effort it demands of you. On God's part, the value of your prayer depends upon the action of the Holy Spirit within you.

Don't dream about praying under ideal conditions. Don't say to yourself: If only I had the time, if only I had peace of mind, if only I could get away from all the hustle-bustle and noise of life! To be sure, you should try to create the best possible exterior conditions for prayer, but, even if you were in the desert, enfolded by complete silence, the main obstacle to prayer would still remain: yourself, and that world of ideas, images, sense impressions, desires . . . which surges within you.

Perhaps you find yourself distracted in prayer. It would be surprising if you didn't. Why do you spend your time at prayer trying to "chase" distractions away? They'll come back again. Rather, recognize them for what they are, look at them calmly whatever they are—serious problems, failings, temptations. Offer them to God in an act of homage asking his forgiveness. Whatever your present circumstances, they should not prevent you from praying, for God is waiting for you. *No one* is ever excluded from prayer. What would you think of someone whose love depended on his digestion, or his feelings, or his successes and failures? Don't let your prayer life depend upon the whims of the moment; make it a regular, daily practice. God is always present, always loving, and he is always waiting for you.

If you were to suggest a subject for a painting to several different artists, the end result would be different in each case. If you carefully observed several different couples, you would find that their love is expressed in quite different ways. The same holds true of prayer; its modes of expression will vary according to cultural influences, age, and temperament. These various modes of expression are not to be despised, each has something to be said for it as a means of communicating with God, but always remember that they are only means. You sin with your whole heart and soul, you love in the same way, you must learn to pray in the same way. Bring your body into prayer as well as your soul, but keep in mind the hierarchical structure of your make-up.[1] Never separate the external gesture from the interior disposition.

Sons can give no greater pleasure to their father than by coming together to show their affection for him. Community prayer and the liturgical prayer of the Church (that is, the official, public prayer of the Church) are not merely optional forms of prayer but the normal mode of expression for the sons of God, all of whom are called to a communal life of love both here and hereafter.

As love deepens, it has less need of gestures and words for self-expression and an increasing need of silence. The same holds true of prayer. As it progresses it becomes more simple. You may find that at times you will not want to say anything at prayer; rather you will find yourself content to sit quietly in silent love. Don't reject this latter form of prayer as being inferior to the former, for the opposite is true.

Perhaps you feel that your prayers are never answered. If so, it's because you have things turned upside down. You ask God that *your* will be done, that *your* plans be accomplished, that he put himself at *your* service. You must adopt just the opposite attitude in prayer. Ask that *his* will be done, that *his* plans be accomplished, that you may put yourself at *his* service. It's not a question of changing God, or of giving him orders; rather it's a matter of changing yourself, of placing yourself completely in his hands. If you want to hear some music on your radio, you first have to turn it on and then dial the right station. If you want to contact God you have to pray, that is, you have to dispose yourself to receive his grace and love.

Nothing is too good for those whom we love. Because his love knows no limits, the Father can not limit his giving to the good things of this earth. His gift is infinite, for it is himself. That's why you should pray that you will pass your exam, or get a salary raise, or succeed in your plans only on condition that it his will, only on condition that it will help you to love him and your brothers more. Be trusting in your prayer. Always place complete trust in God in your prayer. You know that the Father has your best interests at heart, you know that if what you are asking is not for your good his love will answer your prayer accordingly. God has need of your prayer: unless you ask he can not give, for he shows an infinite respect for our freedom in his dealings with us. Silently but incessantly God is asking something of you—your love. Answer his prayer of love.

You can help to spread the spirit of love on earth. You can help to transform the world, but you will accomplish nothing without prayer, for prayer demands that the will of God gradually replace our own, that the love of God gain the ascendency over self-love. Prayer is the means by which the will and love of the Father is mediated to the world of men through us. Sincere and frequent prayer is the foundation stone of your own personal success and that of the world in which you live.

Encounter with Christ in Confession

If there were no such thing as confession, it would have to be invented. . . . And this is precisely what men have done, in their own way. In order to increase production in certain factories in the United States "counsellors" have been offered to the workers in case they might want to talk over problems and worries. What is Marxist "self-criticism" if not a demand for clear recognition of personal failings before pardon is asked for and given? The thousands of letters which pour into the advice-to-the-lovelorn columns of our newspapers and magazines bear witness to a need for confession and an equally urgent need for "spiritual direction." More and more people today, who would never think of kneeling down before a

*priest of God, are enthusiastically giving themselves over
to psychoanalysts.*

*Each of us knows that a host of passions and desires
lurk within, each of us knows the meaning of guilt.
Whether we will or not, each of us is forced to look into
himself from time to time. If a man denies the existence
of God, he can not deny the existence of evil, and if he
refuses to recognize evil as a moral problem, he runs the
risk of ultimate mental illness. Modern man's need for the
psychiatrist is directly related to his rejection of the priest,
but the psychiatrist can never bring true peace, that peace
which Jesus Christ alone offers: "My peace I give unto
you, not as the world gives do I give unto you. . . ."*

*There are two extremes which the Christian must carefully
avoid in his attitude to the sacrament of penance. There
are some for whom the confessional is an anachronism in
modern society, a meaningless ritual to which he submits
himself from time to time so as to satisfy the letter of the
law. On the other hand, there are some who, recognizing
the necessity of the sacrament, approach it out of fear and
for the purpose of regaining a merely human peace of mind.
In both cases, the real meaning of the sacrament of penance
has been perverted for it has been reduced to the plane
of the merely human. It is no longer seen in the light of faith as a
sacramental encounter with Jesus Christ our Redeemer.*

When you approach the sacrament of penance, is your first
thought: What am I going to say? Then do you think:
What will he think of me? And finally: What will he say
to me? Your first thought should be: *Whom* am I going
to encounter in this sacrament, what am I going to *receive*

through it? You give a great deal of attention to the sins which constitute your contribution to the sacrament, but very little to the redemptive love of Christ which constitutes his. Jesus Christ became man, suffered, died and rose from the dead in order to triumph over sin. When we receive the sacrament of penance, we encounter Jesus Christ and we are introduced once again into the mystery of his death and resurrection. Original sin separated man from God and brother from brother. Baptism unites us to Jesus Christ in his redemptive mystery and it is through this encounter that we are made sons of the Father once again and brothers, one of another. Each time you receive the sacrament of penance you choose Jesus Christ as your Redeemer, you are cleansed again as in baptism and you re-establish or strengthen your ties with your Father and your brothers.

It takes an effort to get up each day and start over again. It takes an effort to pick up yesterday's work and start again where you left off. It takes an effort to make sacrifices each day in the name of love. Unfortunately, our rejection of sin and our choice of Jesus Christ are never definitive in this life. Through the medium of the sacrament of penance we must continually return to the option made in baptism in order to renew our decision for Jesus Christ. Why should I bother to go to confession? I know that it will start over again anyway. That's precisely why you do go to confession, for in receiving the sacrament of penance you welcome into your life the power of Christ's victory over death. But, you object: I'll only fall again anyway. If you do fall again, at least you will have the power to make a stepping-stone of your fall. By his death Jesus Christ has won forgiveness for sin for all of us. Hence forgiveness is not something which you must yet win, but rather something which you must gratefully accept from Christ.

The father of the prodigal son stood on a hilltop waiting for his son to return so that he might forgive him. But the son did have to come back in order to receive pardon. God has need of you if he is to fill your heart and the heart of the whole world with his redemptive blessings. We receive only that love which our hearts can hold. We receive only that grace for which our souls have room. The same redemptive blessings are offered to all, but we can receive only those we have opened our hearts to receive. The more acute your sense of sin, the more you will suffer from your failure to love, the more you will long for forgiveness, the more fully will you receive the blessings of the redemption. Why would you bother to look for another answer to your mathematics problem if you din't first realize that your first was wrong. Why would you bother to turn back if you hadn't first discovered that you were on the wrong road? Jesus Christ, by his death on the cross, has already taken away your sins. But precisely because you are free, you must give your sins to him. You must first recognize and accept your sins for what they are before you can give them to Christ, your Redeemer. A mysterious exchange takes place in the confessional: you give all your sins to Jesus Christ and he pours out on you all the blessings of the redemption.

If you only check your bookkeeping once a year, you're going to have quite a bit of trouble trying to locate your errors. If you only examine your conscience once a year, you won't be able to lay bare all your failings. Some people, because they are insensitive to the feelings of others, wound them without even realizing it. If you do not see your failings, it's because you don't pay enough attention to what you're doing, but, even more so, it's because your love doesn't penetrate deeply enough. If you want to make a good examination of conscience, you must first place yourself in the presence of God and then in the presence of yourself. Sin can be appreciated for what it really is only if it is seen against the holiness of God: "... sin displeases *You*...." You will come to know yourself only if you have accustomed yourself to reviewing your life in the light of faith.[1] Once you have come to see Jesus Christ present in your life inviting you to union with him through the circumstances of this life, you will then see more clearly how often you have refused these invitations. You can see the evil you've done; try to see the good you've failed to do as well. The deeper your love, the more clearly you will see your lack of love.

Sin involves not only separation from God but separation from all our brothers in the Church. Your return to the life of the community must be publicly acknowledged in the Church and not simply in the hidden recesses of your heart. You confess your sins not only to God alone, but "to the Blessed Virgin Mary ... to all the saints and to you, Father ... ," That is, to the priest who is Christ's minister and the representative of the community. Would you refuse a gift because you didn't like the person who was offering it to you? What difference does it make who the priest is who hears your confession, for he holds in his hands the fruits of the death and resurrection of Jesus Christ? You certainly have the right to choose your own confessor, but you can never avoid going to confession simply because you are afraid of the priest or because you don't like him.

Within the context of the Mystical Body of Christ, whatever we do, for good or ill, influences the life of all the other members of this Body. When we receive the sacrament of penance, we hold out to all our brothers the grace of a personal renewal in their own lives. Through this sacrament you mediate Jesus Christ in his redemptive mystery to those with whom Providence brings you into contact. In making yourself present through genuine concern to those with whom you live and work, you are able, through the sacrament of penance, to bring their sins to Christ and you are also able to bring Christ's redemptive blessings to them. In your struggles against social injustice, broken homes, neighbourhood conflict and hostility, war, unjust wages, slums, illiteracy, hunger . . . never forget that all these evils are the result of sin and that sin can be overcome only by the divine Redeemer. If you content yourself with confessing your sins without struggling against sin in yourself and in the world in which you live, you will never overcome evil. If you content yourself with struggling against the evil in yourself and in the world in which you live without confessing your sins, you will never win your struggle. The only infallible means of overcoming sin is personal struggle against all its wiles and disguises at the same time that you welcome into your life —through the sacrament of penance—Jesus Christ, the Lamb who has vanquished evil.

No Room
for Discouragement

*Why do some become discouraged in the long struggle
against the forces of sin? Either because they find
themselves continually confronted by the same problems
from which they see no possible exit, or because they find
themselves falling over and over again when they had
thought the victory won. In both cases we see a lack of
confidence in the all-powerful love of God. Discouragement
can warp the whole of our lives, and because it is essentially
a lack of confidence it leads us further and further from
the Lord who alone has power to redeem us.
Discouragement should find no place in the life of the
Christian, for Jesus Christ has conquered sin and
death for us all.*

Everything is going badly for you; your life is one long
series of regrets; nothing seems worthwhile to you any
more. You've given up trying: What's the use, I'll never
be able to solve my problems, there's no hope. Discouragement has completely paralyzed you; you refuse to fight
back any more, you no longer have the upper hand, you're
just living your life out now without purpose or hope. If
you're discouraged, it's because you put all your trust in
your own efforts and now you realize that you can't go
it alone. Had you placed your trust in God, you would still
feel regret for your failings, but you wouldn't be discouraged. You forget that God is as loving and as all-
powerful after you've fallen as before. Discouragement is

clear proof that you've placed too much confidence in yourself and too little in God.

Don't try to gloss over your failings and sins: if only I could have prevented that; if only I could go back; if only I could start all over again; I can't understand why I should have so many problems; it's not fair; it's all a matter of temperament so what can I do about it? If you really want to overcome sin, you first have to recognize that you are a sinner. Don't try to cover it over, don't look for excuses or try to forget about it, or deny it, for if you do, you're closing the door to the truth about yourself. Learn to accept your failures, your difficulties, your habits of sin, those occasions of sin which you can not escape.

Jesus Christ has not come to take away all our temptations, nor to eliminate the possibility of sin, rather he has come to take away the sins of the world. The saints themselves were not exempted from the struggle against evil. St Paul in his Epistle to the Romans underlines this fact: 'For I do not understand what I do, for it is not what I wish that I do, but what I hate, that I do. . . . For I do not the good that I wish, but the evil that I do not wish, that I perform. . . . For I am delighted with the law of God according to the inner man, but I see another law in my members, warring against the law of my mind and making me prisoner to the law of sin that is in my members. Unhappy man that I am: Who will deliver me from the body of this death?'[1]

In the eyes of God, the real value of a man is not to be measured by the ineffectual character of his temptations, or the infrequency of his falls, or even the absence of materially grave sin, but rather first and foremost by his complete confidence in his all-powerful Saviour, by his love, and by his determination to keep on trying in spite of failures. As long as traces of discouragement and melancholy persist in your attitude to yourself and your world, you do not yet trust completely in the compassion and forgiveness of the Lord, for the thought of his mercy should fill you with peace and joy.

When the prodigal son returned home, his father wanted nothing more than that the past be forgotten. He ordered a feast so that all might rejoice with him. 'There is more joy in heaven over one sinner who repents than over ninety-nine just who have no need of repentance.' Jesus Christ hates sin but generously and even lavishly shows pity to the sinner. If you have sinned, the Lord comes to you to show you his love and to offer you his redemptive mercy: the incomprehensible mystery of God's love for man. All things work together unto good for those who love God, even sin. Each fall is a sign, an invitation, to offer yourself to your Saviour.

You know your own weakness only too well, you see yourself at the mercy of every onslaught of temptation. Your egocentricity and selfishness seem to be gaining the ascendency rather than decreasing. You are even more acutely aware now of your failure to love. Don't give way to discouragement; rather, rejoice, for the Lord came to save sinners and not the just. If you surrender yourself to him, he will forgive you and lead you to salvation. How can you ask for forgiveness if you do not see the evil which is present in your life? Why should you come to Jesus Christ in search of salvation if you experience no need for salvation? You will not find peace of mind through greater self-assurance, through a misplaced trust in your own virtue. This kind of peace of mind is pure illusion, for it implies that you no longer have any need of Jesus Christ, and you will find yourself alone, terribly alone and terribly vulnerable, without him. 'I have not come to save the just but the sinner.' 'I have come to save what was lost.' 'It's not those who are well who have need of the physician but those who are sick.'

Be particularly wary of that type of discouragement which can arise out of sins against purity. Sins of this kind can create a feeling of emptiness and malaise which, coupled with a fear of having become the slave of instinct, can lead you to exaggerate your actual situation. Sins of weakness are not to be equated in gravity with sins against faith, hope, and love. A habit of sin restricts the exercise of your freedom, but it also limits your responsibility. If a habit of sin has caught you in its grip, you will have to win back your freedom, but be patient. You shouldn't be discouraged by your own weakness if you recognize at the same time that God's grace is sufficient for you. The grace of God will never fail you but you have to open yourself to receive it. There are two perversions of the Christian moral life which have to be guarded against: staying down once you've fallen and sitting by the side of the road thinking that you've already reached your destination. Your failings should make you recognize your own weakness; they will help you to become a little child again and to place your hand in the Father's as you make your way to your eternal destination.

'I keep the Lord always within my sight; for he is at my right hand, I shall not be moved, For this reason my heart is glad and my soul rejoices; moreover my body also will rest secure.'[2]

The Unfathomable Mystery
of the Mass

The Mass is for the Christian an unfathomable mystery of faith. We must, therefore, not seek to reduce it to our own human categories. The Mass is situated at the very heart of our supernatural destiny and is for the Christian the inexhaustible and unique source of salvation, for it makes present again the saving mystery of Christ's death and resurrection. Through it Jesus Christ each day pours out on the world the blessings of the new creation.

What place does the Mass occupy in your life? Is it a long bore, or a meaningless formalism, or an onerous duty, or perhaps a welcome rest from the cares of the world, or one devotional exercise among many, or a mere esthetic experience? How do you occupy your time at Mass? Do you watch the priest, with admiration if he's a friend or with a critical eye if he's not? Do you listen to the singing and watch the 'ceremony' as if you were in a theatre? Perhaps you spend your time admiring the vestments and the decorations, or perhaps you take advantage of the opportunity for 'quiet meditation' or for some form of prayer. Perhaps you enjoy the sermon and spend your time thinking about it during Mass. It may be that you know a little something about the Mass from frequent participation in it, but you're disappointed when Father so-and-so doesn't say it because he says Mass so much better than . . . , you prefer a certain parish because . . . , you don't really feel as if you've been to Mass when. . . .

Thus in various and sundry ways the mind of man is

able to reduce the Holy Sacrifice of the Mass to the level of mere ceremonial splendour, or to make of it one form of devotion among many others meant for the private edification of the individual. You haven't really even scratched the veneer, you're leaving aside the real heart of the Mass's meaning because you don't approach the Mass as a sacred event, which is precisely what it is. In the Mass, man, now a partaker of the very life of God, a son of God, participates at this moment in history, together with the whole Body of Christ, in the central event of human history. This event is the reconciliation of man and his world with the Father through the mediatorial sacrifice of Jesus Christ, God made man. Through the Mass you are brought into contact with the Christian mystery in all its profundity and richness.[1]

THE REDEMPTION OF THE WORLD

Man and the world in which he lives, both made by the loving God, can attain total fulfilment only by returning to the Father through a generous response of love to his call of love. Original sin and all of our own person sins constitute man's refusal to respond to this call. With the rejection of God man's life becomes self-centred and man becomes the god of creation. In making himself a god man destroys the order of reality, introducing not only conflict but suffering and death as well.[2] Had man not introduced sin into God's creation, his offering of himself and the world in which he lives would have been made to God in peace and joy. Because of sin, man's offering involves abnegation and detachment; it thus becomes a sacrifice made at the cost of suffering—an immolation.

Right from the very beginning, man, repentant and

afraid, has tried to re-establish the broken covenant-relation with God by offering sacrifice. These sacrifices, however, proved infinitely inadequate. The whole of the human family was caught up in Adam's refusal, for by one man's sin death came into the world for all. And so another came, Jesus Christ by name, who made a New Covenant between man and the Father. Jesus Christ, because he is God, because the lives and sufferings of all men have been gathered together in his life and suffering, offers a perfect sacrifice to the Father. The Father accepts the sacrifice of his Son, and, through the Resurrection, he reveals his forgiveness of sinful humanity. This life of the risen Christ is then communicated to the human family through the Church, his Body. The redemption, the true Passover, is now an accomplished fact [3] and entrance into the Promised Land (that is, heaven) is guaranteed.

Jesus Christ, the first-born of many brethren, Head of the Mystical Body, has entered once and for all into heavenly glory as victorious King. Through him, man lives with God; through him even the material has been elevated to participation in God's life in some mysterious way. Man and his world are now on their way to final resurrection. Jesus Christ, risen from the dead, becomes for us a tangible promise of everlasting life and in him the whole of creation has been caught up in the ascending movement of salvation.

THE MASS: THE SACRIFICE OF CHRIST

The mere existence of a road doesn't necessarily mean that it will be taken. Being carried along by the crowd is not to be compared with a clearly chosen way of life. Man is distinguishable from the world in which he lives because of his personal freedom and so in order to give us the opportunity to unite ourselves freely with his redemptive sacrifice, Jesus Christ has provided a means of making his sacrifice present to all men, of every age and of every nation. Because he could not make his sacrifice present in the form which it took on Calvary, he instituted, at the Last Supper, a new form, a sacramental form, which we call the Mass.[4] In the Mass, the Church, through the ministry of her priests, makes present, here and now, the sacrifice of the Cross—so that each individually and all together can offer this sacrifice to the Father, in a spirit of adoration and praise, throughout the whole course of human history—so that each individually and all together can unite themselves to this sacrifice by offering themselves and the whole human family, while applying to themselves the redemptive blessings of Jesus Christ by receiving his Body in the Eucharist.

THE OFFERTORY

In the Holy Sacrifice of the Mass the bread and wine offered by the whole community symbolize the return of the whole created order to its Creator: the wheat transformed the minerals of the earth and the rays of the sun into its own life, the farmer sowed the seed, the farmer's tractor was built by a large manufacturer, the iron ore for it was mined in Minnesota, a mining engineer directed the mining operation. . . . Present in these grains of wheat and drops of wine is the whole of creation in its mysterious longing to attain life, the whole of the human family in its effort to bring creation to fulfilment. The whole cosmos, the whole human family are there together, each needing the other for its completion; the whole created order, man and his world, man with all his joys and sorrows, is present in the sacrifice of the Mass. As you offer the bread and the wine and all that they symbolize you will come to recognize that the whole material order, that all life, and especially your own life, belong to God. The sacrifice of the Mass, then, encompasses the whole of reality.

The hand which is offered in friendship represents a total personal gift of self. A kiss is a sign of love's gift. When you participate in the sacrifice of the Mass you are the hands, the heart, the lips of all the human family; by your personal fiat to the Word of God you offer the whole cosmos to God; in the Mass you pray with and for your brothers and perhaps in their place: Lord, behold our sufferings, our sins, our love, our lives. If you seek to make the most of the grace of the present moment, to elevate the material world by your daily work, to develop every aspect of your personality, to make your life and the lives of those around you lives of love, to take your part in the struggle for social justice, personal freedom, and world peace, to cultivate a spirit of brotherhood in your relations with your world, to be more detached, more available to others, more open to the world about you and beyond you, you will have that much more to offer to Christ the High Priest. Our Lord depends upon us to continue throughout the whole course of history his sacrifice of love, offered once and for all to the Father. We can only continue his sacrifice by uniting ourselves with it. You must learn to make each moment of your day a more intense offertory of love.

THE CONSECRATION

Your arms aren't long enough to carry your gift to God. Your heart isn't pure enough to offer a selfless gift to God.

You have need of the Church's priests to speak to God for you, to speak to you of God, to be other Christs in the midst of the community of the Church. You need the priest to speak the words of Consecration over your offering and that of the whole human family: This is my body, this is my blood. At the Consecration you place the bread and wine in the hands of Jesus Christ so that he can make them his own sacrifice. The Lord—through the lips of the priest—effects the profoundest of transformations, reaching to the very substance of the bread and wine, drawing it in fact into the mystery of redemption. An incomprehensible change takes place at the Consecration, for matter becomes not only humanized but even divinized. Through the risen Christ, matter shares in the glory of the resurrection. Through this transformation of the bread and the wine, man and his world are taken up by Jesus Christ to be offered, redeemed and saved.

If you give something which you prize to one of your brothers, it necessarily involves a sacrifice. In giving some of your money or your time or something of *yourself* to one of your brothers you make a still greater sacrifice. In giving the whole of your life to one of your brothers you make the supreme sacrifice. As a baptized Christian, you have infinite power over the heart of your heavenly Father, for Baptism confers upon you a priestly power, a power to offer the infinitely pleasing sacrifice of his Son, Jesus Christ.

THE COMMUNION

Having offered the sacrifice of Jesus Christ to the Father, you are invited by him to share in your own redemption by receiving your Saviour. Thanks to the Eucharist, the death and resurrection of Christ cease to be merely a historical event situated in the distant past. Jesus Christ ceases to be identifiable with a particular country or race or social class or historical period. Jesus Christ and his sacrifice are made contemporary by the sacrifice of the Mass and the Eucharist.

Love always seeks complete union, complete identification. Jesus Christ has chosen to make himself and his redemptive sacrifice present to the world under the appearances of bread so that you can be nourished by his love and transformed into himself. When you encounter the risen Christ in the Eucharist you are welcoming the redemptive mystery into your life, you are freeing yourself still more from the fetters of sin, you are being transformed into a son of God, a partaker of the life of Christ. However, the Eucharist is not merely a private affair; it is meant to be a means of bringing the blessings of Christ's redemptive sacrifice into your neighbourhood, into your work, and into your relations with others. You are a unique and irreplaceable actor in the drama of human history, and Jesus Christ has need of you to make his salvific work present in this particular place, at this particular moment of history. If, when you receive the Eucharist, you are consciously present to the totality of your life-situation, you become one more mediator through whom the world is incorporated into the movement of salvation history. You become a source of eternal life for the body of humanity. You become a source of new strength for the life of the Mystical Body of Christ.

You are not authentically entering into union with Jesus Christ in the Eucharist if you knowingly and willingly refuse to develop the whole of your personality; if you are habitually unscrupulous in your business or professional practice; if you refuse to work, living solely from the work of others; if, through selfishness, you refuse to take part in the struggle for social justice and world peace; if you refuse to love; if you refuse to bring new life into the world when it lies within your means to do so; if you refuse to have anything at all to do with one of your brothers. For when you receive the Eucharist you encounter not only the physical body of Jesus Christ but his Mystical Body as well; you are brought into contact with the whole Christ, Head and members, that is, with all men who are your brothers, those in heaven as well as those on earth, with the whole cosmos.

The work of redemption has already been accomplished by Jesus Christ, but you prevent its full accomplishment in your own life by refusing to unite the whole of your life to the perfect offering of Jesus Christ, and by refusing to welcome Jesus Christ into every aspect of your life. The Mass is the sacramental act by which the whole of creation is transformed in Jesus Christ. Through it the Church elevates the whole cosmos and the whole of the human family; through it the ascending movement of human history towards God in Christ is accomplished. 'It remains for you to bring your life to this sacrifice, to make your activity in the world and that of your brothers nothing less than the saving action of the Man-God.'5 When all has been completed, when man collaborating with God has brought creation to fulfilment, when Christ is 'all in all,' when the Mystical Body has attained its full maturity, when the blessings of the redemption have been communicated to all and Christ has gathered all together into one fold, then the Church will cease its celebration of the Eucharistic mystery, it will cease recalling under a sacramental form the death and resurrection of the Lord, for he will come in his own person with the sacramental veil drawn back. Then the whole Christ, Head and members, will be presented to the Father from the pierced but radiant hands of the Redeemer. Then the liturgy of unending thanksgiving will burst forth from the redeemed hearts of humanity and the whole of creation, man and his world, will have attained fulfilment.

Love is from God

All genuine love sets man on the road leading to God, for as St John tells us 'love is from God.'[1] Even though love, at the level of man's natural powers, is already an opening onto the infinite, it still demands complete surrender to the love of Jesus Christ if it is to find fulfilment in the supernatural. The Christian possesses an extraordinary power, for the life of grace enables him to love God and his brothers as God loves himself and his sons.

It is impossible that by nature man suffers hunger without hope of food, or thirst without hope of drink, or have a question without hope of an answer, or crave love without hope of love. Man's quest for fulfilment is a never-ending search. The foundation stone of your desire to love and to be loved in return is your radical incompleteness, and it is precisely through love that you seek to overcome this incompleteness. However, this indefatigable quest for the union which love effects will leave you profoundly dissatisfied so long as the God who is love has not yet filled your need. Love involves, in its very essence, a quest and this quest is ultimately for God. Because love has the power to take us out of ourselves it has, at the same time, the power to bring us nearer to God, for man's love is confronted with but two basic alternatives: self or the other (and ultimately, the Other). It is impossible for us not to centre our lives on love, for the God who is love has loved us from all eternity and love calls forth love. You are beloved of the loving God and your life must be a reply of love.

The heart of the revelation made in Jesus Christ is that God is love and that salvation history is a history of love at work in the world and that the final consummation will be the fruit of love's labours. Genuine love is always the sign of God's presence, for God is present in love as the sun is present in each of its rays. 'Love is from God. And everyone who loves is born of God and knows God. He who does not love does not know God, for God is love. . . . He who abides in love abides in God and God in him.'[2] You can see God present in the world, in all the many diverse expressions of genuine love. You can bring God into your world through self-forgetfulness and the gift of self to others. You can bring others to God by helping them to love their brothers. In every expression of your love you bear witness to Love, quietly but eloquently you proclaim the Lord Jesus Christ's coming. It is your mission in the world to reveal love as Someone.

As we grow in love we approach closer to God and hence each new love should be seen as an opportunity to deepen our union with the Son of God: the awakening of love in adolescence, the discovery of the meaning of self-giving, friendship, engagement, marriage, father-hood and motherhood, the struggle for a better world in which to live. Our lives are literally filled with oppor-tunities for giving: at home, at work, at play. The God who is love continually offers us the chance to live by and for love alone. In the night-time of life we shall be judged on love alone. Love comes from God and leads infallibly back to him; but if you think that you've already reached your destination, if you stop when you're only halfway there, if you pervert love into an adventure in self-seeking, then your journey to God will come to an abrupt stop because you have made a god of that which is merely a way to the one, true God. This is nothing more than idolatry, pure and simple. Your self-created gods hide the one, true God from view and unless you start over again on your way to this God, you are condemning yourself to gnawing dissatisfaction and, what is even worse, you are making your ultimate fulfilment an impossibility.

Love always seeks complete union with the beloved. Man is only too painfully aware that such union is un-attainable in this life. If you would attain love's goal, you must welcome God into your life and he will unite you with those whom you love. Could you rest content with a qualified offer of love: I will love you until such-and-such a day, I love you but I will only make certain sacrifices? True love demands the infinite and only God can satisfy such a demand. Ask your beloved if she loves the God who is love. If she replies 'yes,' then you can rest assured that her love will know no qualifications or reservations. If, however, her answer is 'no,' her love will fall infinitely short of love's needs. Your heart is much too small to contain the infinite God, it is even too small to open out to embrace all your brothers with God's own love, and yet it is precisely this love which God expects of you. Your brothers are looking not simply for love from you, but for a divine love.

Your love has to be not merely *natural* but *supernatural* in character. You stand in continual need of the redemptive and purifying love of Christ if your love is to be saved from egoism. You stand in continual need of the love of Christ if your love is to be made divine. The theological virtue of charity is in fact simply the mysterious power, communicated by grace, to love as God loves, to love with the heart of Christ. It is this love which embraces God, your Father, and all men, your brothers. If you would love more fully, let the God of love come more fully into your life, let this God love in and through you. Let God's love for his sons be manifested in your love for your brothers, his sons. If you love the other with a natural love, you will unite him to yourself; but if you love him in the spirit of charity, you will unite him to Christ. If you love in and with Christ, you are helping to bring the Mystical Body to completion, you are helping to extend the Father's kingdom at the same time that you proclaim its reality. It's not a question of *doing what's charitable* but of *being love*. In the wonderful expression of St Ausgustine: 'Love and do what you will.'

References

A MAN HAS TO STAND ON HIS FEET
[1]If we make use of the term 'level' in respect to man, it is for the purpose of underlining the respective value of the various elements which go into his make-up; however, we must never lose sight of the fact that man is a unified whole and that he commits himself as a whole in each of his acts. (Cf. 'The Divided Man,' p. 12)
[2]Cf. 'The Well-Ordered Man,' p. 15

THE TWO DIMENSIONS OF MAN
[1]Gal. 2: 20
[2]Gen. 11: 8
[3]I John 3: 14

THE DIVIDED MAN
[1]'A Man has to Stand on his Feet,' p. 3
[2]Cf. 'How to Concentrate,' p. 83

THE WELL-ORDERED MAN
[1]Cf. 'A Man has to Stand on his Feet,' p. 3
[2]'At the basis of human emotions we find a certain physical sensitivity which allows the individual to be affected by external stimuli which are quite subtle in character and even unapparent . . . at times you find yourself overcome by a sort of interior confusion which reason is quite incapable of subduing.' Louis Lavelle, L'erreur de Narcisse, p. 89.
[3]Cf. 'A Man has to Stand on his Feet,' p. 3
[4]If possible, write down the results of this 'exercise.' Try it two or three times a week.
[5]'The surprising thing about emotion is that it seems to be an end in which the soul finds rest: instead it is a movement designed to awaken the soul to activity...' Louis Lavelle, op. cit., p. 91
[6]Ps. 36: 4

THE VOCATION OF WOMAN
[1]Gal. 3: 28
[2]Gen. 2: 28

VOCATION OF THE SINGLE WOMAN
[1]We are not speaking in this chapter of those whose celibate life has been freely chosen or of those who are celibate as a result of their choice of the religious life. The first case is extremely rare and the second requires special consideration.

VOCATION OF THE SINGLE WOMAN—*continued*
[2]*Gen.* 2: 18. Cf. 'Adolescence: Preparation for Love,' p. 32.
[3]*Gen.* 2: 24
[4]Cf. I *Cor.* 7: 27, 33-4, 37-8
[5]To gain your own independence, to love your parents as an adult and not as a child, to help them to realize that their child is a person enjoying full autonomy, does not mean to abandon one's family. You must help them financially, you must show your love for them and even take care of them if need be, but all the while gaining and maintaining your full personal freedom as an adult. This applies to married children as well, but it is easy to see that it is much more difficult for the single person to achieve maturity, especially if he lives at home. [6]It is a very serious mistake for the single girl to think that she has to live at home with her family. Many young women have in this way effectively hampered their personal development.
[7]Cf. 'The Vocation of Woman,' p. 20
[8]Membership in a group of devout Christians is an invaluable support for those whose faith finds expression in commitment to work in the world; it is an invaluable source of strength for this work. However, such a group can pose a serious threat to individual members when it becomes—unconsciously perhaps—a defence mechanism against a life of solitude which has not been made fruitful through an effective concern for others. The emotions find a dangerous kind of satisfaction in this contact with 'kindred spirits' and with a priest whom one greatly admires. The members may indeed find one another's company mutually edifying; they are sincerely convinced that these circumstances are truly sanctifying for them; however, by cutting themselves off from their more apostolic brothers who are labouring in the front lines, they may be thwarting all possibility of authentic spiritual maturity.

ADOLESCENCE: PREPARATION FOR LOVE
[1]*Gen.* 2: 18
[2]Because of the basic lack of insight upon which such a marriage is built it is rare indeed that even the most elementary conditions necessary for a stable marriage are realized. Later on in life, when the partners have reached adult life and see things more clearly, they will find it extremely difficult to accept such a union graciously. All too often a broken home results from the union of two physically, or at least psychologically, immature adolescents.

MAN AND TECHNOLOGY
[1]It should be made clear at this point that we are not opposed to salary increases; what is involved here is the inordinate attachment to material goods and the desire to have more and more.
[2]*Gen.* 11: 4
[3]I *Cor.* 7: 30-1
[4]Cf. 'A Man has to Stand on his Feet,' p. 3

THE DIVINE VOCATION OF MAN
[1]Cf. 'Man and Technology,' p. 37
[2]*Eph.* 1: 3-6
[3]Cf. 'Encounter with Christ in Confession,' p. 185
[4]Faith, hope, and charity are the new 'faculties' of your supernatural life.
[5]Cf. 'A Man has to Stand on his Feet,' p. 3
[6]*Gal.* 2: 20
[7]Cf. 'The Divided Man,' p. 12
[8]*Eph.* 1: 10
[9]Cf. 'The two Dimensions of Man,' p. 7

CAST YOUR CARE UPON THE LORD
[1]*Ps.* 30: 6
[2]*Ps.* 4: 9
[3]*Ps.* 54: 23

HOW TO BE FREE
[1]Cf. 'A Man has to Stand on his Feet,' p. 3

HOW TO BE BEAUTIFUL
[1]'. . . Our form is moulded by our physiological habits and even by our usual thoughts . . . The shape of the face, the mouth, the cheeks, the eyelids, and the lines of the visage are determined by the habitual condition of the flat muscles, which move in the adipose tissue underlying the skin. And the state of these muscles depends on that of our mind . . . Unwittingly, our visage progressively models itself upon our state of consciousness. With the advance of age it becomes more and more pregnant with the feelings, the appetites, and the aspirations of the whole being. . . . ' Alexis Carrel: *Man, The Unknown,* p. 63.

HOW NOT TO BE BUSY
[1]'How to Concentrate,' p. 83 and 'The Grace of the Present Moment,' p. 89.

STOP FOR A MOMENT
[1]Cf. 'The Divided Man,' p. 12

REFLECT, EVALUATE, DECIDE
[1]Cf. 'Accepting Yourself as You Are,' p. 49

HOW TO CONCENTRATE
[1]Cf. 'The Divided Man,' p. 12
[2]Cf. 'How not to be Busy,' p. 70

MAN'S WORK IN THE WORLD
[1]Cf. 'Reflect, Evaluate, Decide,' p. 78
[2]Cf. 'Reviewing your Personal Life,' p. 168
[3]Cf. 'Reviewing your Personal Life,' p. 168, and 'Reviewing your Group Life,' p. 171

HOW TO TALK TO OTHERS
[1]Cf. 'Cast your Care upon the Lord,' p. 58

THE ENCOUNTER IN DIALOGUE
[1]Cf. 'Who is the Other?' p. 93
[2]Cf. 'The Double Point of View,' p. 151

HOW TO HELP OTHERS
[1]*Rom.* 5: 20

WHAT IS LOVE?
[1]The role of feeling in human life is discussed in the chapter entitled: 'The Well-Ordered Man,' p. 15
[2]Renunciation, if it is to bear fruit, has to be *positive,* thus involving the opening out of the personality through gift-giving. Cf. 'The Well-Ordered Man,' p. 15.
[3]Cf. 'The two Dimensions of Man,' p. 7

WHAT DOES IT MEAN TO LOVE?
[1]Cf. 'What is Love?' p. 108

WHAT DOES IT MEAN TO BE MARRIED?
[1]Cf. 'A Man has to Stand on his Feet,' p. 3
[2]Cf. 'No Room for Discouragement,' p. 186

WHEN IS THREE A CROWD?
[1]Cf. 'Accepting Yourself as You Are,'p. 47

THE MYSTERY OF SUFFERING
[1]*Rom.* 6: 23

MAN: COLLABORATOR WITH GOD
[1]When in this chapter we refer to the creative aspects of man's nature we mean procreative (that is, creative together with God). Properly speaking, man is never creative (that is, he never makes something out of nothing).
[2]This does not mean simply the physical birth of the child but his psychological birth as well, that is, sorrow will accompany the process of education and development.

YOUR COMMITMENT TO OTHERS
[1]Cf. *Luke* 10: 25-37; *Matt.* 25: 31-46
[2]Cf. 'A Man has to Stand on his Feet,' p. 3
[3]'The two Dimensions of Man,' p. 7
[4]An extract from the Rule of the Companions of Emmaus which appeared in the periodical, *Faim et Soif*.

YOU ARE YOUR BROTHER'S KEEPER
[1]Cf. *L'Abbé Pierre vous parle*, Editions Le Centurion (Bonne Presse); *Emmaus* 1959, by Abbé Pierre, Editions du Soleil Levant.
[2]*Gen.* 4: 10
[3]Abbé Pierre
[4]Abbé Pierre
[5]Abbé Pierre
[6]Abbé Pierre
[7]*Matt.* 25: 31-46

THE DOUBLE POINT OF VIEW
[1]*John* 8: 12

SEEK OUT JESUS CHRIST
[1]*John* 6: 44
[2]*Gal.* 5: 6

THE ENCOUNTER WITH JESUS CHRIST
[1]This indictment is not meant to imply that scientific study of the gospels is to be ignored; such study is necessary. This approach, however, does not *directly* aim at nourishing the spiritual life which is the point in question here.
[2]*Heb.* 1: 1
[3]*Heb.* 4: 12
[4]Charles de Foucauld
[5]It is assumed of course that you all have personally meditated on the gospel passage assigned during the past week or two.

REVIEWING YOUR PERSONAL LIFE
[1]If possible, it would be useful to write down your observations, at least at first.
[2]Cf. 'The Grace of the Present Moment,' p. 86, and 'Reflect, Evaluate, Decide,' p. 75
[3]Examination of conscience has reference obviously to the conscience and hence to the moral value of our acts. The review of which we speak has reference to life: its purpose is to enable us to contact Jesus Christ who manifests himself through the exigencies of our concrete situation in the world.
[4]Cf. 'The Double Point of View,' p. 151. This review is not a matter of merely human reflection; rather it takes its inspiration from a Christian faith seeking to understand Christian life in the world more profoundly. It is essentially religious in character in much the same way that, for example, mental prayer is.
[5]Cf. 'The Encounter with Jesus Christ,' p. 158

REVIEWING YOUR GROUP LIFE

1Action implies not only personal effort but an attempt to get others to make an effort on their own behalf.

PRAYER IS AN ACT OF FAITH

1Cf. 'A Man has to Stand on his Feet,' p. 3

ENCOUNTER WITH CHRIST IN CONFESSION

1Cf. 'Reviewing your Personal Life,' p. 168

NO ROOM FOR DISCOURAGEMENT

1*Rom.* 7: 15–24
2*Ps.* 15: 8–9

THE UNFATHOMABLE MYSTERY OF THE MASS

1It seems advisable at this point to recall a remark made in the Introduction: we have no intention in these chapters of offering an exhaustive study of each question discussed, merely some reflections on certain aspects of each.
2Cf. 'The Mystery of Suffering,' p. 123
3On the feast of the Passover the Jews celebrated their passage through the Red Sea from slavery in Egypt to a new life as God's people. The Passover for the Christian consists in his liberation by Christ from the slavery of sin.
4A Sacrament is a visible sign, or symbol, which effects what it signifies and signifies what it effects.
5Père Lebret: *Principes pour l'Action.*

LOVE IS FROM GOD

1*I John* 4:7
2*I John* 4: 7–8, 16